MY
▶▶▶▶▶▶▶▶▶▶▶▶▶▶▶▶▶▶▶▶▶▶
BOOK
OF
MORMON
▶▶▶▶▶▶▶▶▶▶▶▶▶▶▶▶▶▶▶▶▶▶

STUDY GUIDE
DIAGRAMS, DOODLES, & INSIGHTS

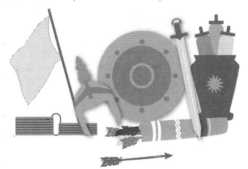

ALMA –MORONI

THIS BOOK BELONGS TO: _____

© The Red Headed Hostess LLC
www.theredheadedhostess.com

i

OTHER BOOKS
BY
SHANNON FOSTER

DOCTRINE & COVENANTS STUDY BOOK

This is a study book for adults or youths who want to dive deep into their scriptures. This book is designed to help you to study section by section, and scripture by scripture. Each page has a template you can fill in as you study. These templates are carefully designed to help you get the most out of your study and have a place to record the doctrines and principles you study.

* See more at
www.theredheadedhostess.com

NAMES OF CHRIST STUDY BOOK

Have you ever taken the time to study the names of Christ that are found in the scriptures? In this study journal, there are over 70 names that you can look up, consider, and write about. Each page has a guided outline that you can fill in to aid your study experience, all in the hopes of understanding the Savior better.

* See more at
www.theredheadedhostess.com

YOUNG WOMEN VALUES DOODLE JOURNAL

This 240-page Young Women Doodle Journal is designed to help your young women get the most out of their Personal Progress program! There are pages for all 7 experiences for each of the eight Young Women values - so a total of 56 scripture and application experiences! In this journal the girls can "doodle" what they are learning from each scripture, talk, book, and document they are asked to study.

* See more at:
www.theredheadedhostess.com

SCRIPTURE STUDY JOURNAL - CHAPTERS-

It is so important to write down what you are learning so you will never forget! This is a study journal to help you study and record what you are learning in your scriptures as you study individual CHAPTERS.

As you study chapter-by-chapter, there is a basic outline on each page that allows you to write down things such as: words you looked up, significant doctrines and principles you found, questions you asked, your own personal thoughts and insights, and more! Start now and record all of the amazing things the scriptures are teaching you right now in your life! Plus... what amazing gift to leave your posterity!

* See more at
www.theredheadedhostess.com

SCRIPTURE STUDY JOURNAL - TOPICS -

It is so important to write down what you are learning so you will never forget! This is a study journal to help you study and record what you are learning in your scriptures as you study individual TOPICS.

As you study various TOPICS, there is a basic outline on each page that allows you to write down things such as: definitions, scriptures that teach about that topic, favorite quotes, and your own personal thoughts and insights.

There is also a companion journal available that helps you focus on individual CHAPTERS. The two journals are complimentary in nature and organized in a way that you can reference your journals to each other.

BECOMING LIKE MY SCRIPTURE HERO

Have you ever imagined what your favorite scripture heros would be like if they lived in today's world? This book is a day-by-day study of principles and standards where you can imagine what they might be like and how you can become more like them! You will fill this book with thoughts, insights, quotes, and scriptures. Use this along with your scripture study and see how your hero will become very real to you and a true friend.

* See more at
www.theredheadedhostess.com

* MORE BOOKS FOUND
AT
WWW.THEREDHEADEDHOSTESS.COM

TABLE OF CONTENTS

INSTRUCTIONS

WHAT IS A DOODLE?

For the sake of this scripture journal, doodles are any drawing, word, diagram, etc. that comes to your mind as you are studying. This journal is a place for you to study the Book of Mormon and fill it with anything that helps you learn, understand, and record!

With a doodle journal, you can be as creative as you want as you study. Everyone's journal should be different!

For example, see the excerpts below that all come from this scripture journal. See how different they can be!

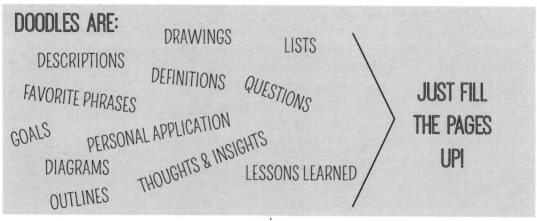

DOODLES ARE:

DRAWINGS   LISTS
DESCRIPTIONS
    DEFINITIONS   QUESTIONS
FAVORITE PHRASES
GOALS   PERSONAL APPLICATION
DIAGRAMS   THOUGHTS & INSIGHTS   LESSONS LEARNED
OUTLINES

JUST FILL THE PAGES UP!

SAMPLE PAGES

MY COMMENTARY

SCRIPTURE/
PAGE

1 Nephi 1:18-20 Page 9	I never thought or realized what a courageous man Lehi was. I wonder what kind of life he had lived to qualify to be chosen for such an assignment! Also, he must have had fears and concerns - but he did it anyway!
	Maybe that is what true disciples are. They go forth despite fear ; and as they go forth in the strength of the Lord, they are led and guided to do amazing things. If Lehi was too worried or self-conscious, we probably would never even know his name! What an example he is to all of us!
	I want to be more like Lehi!!! Next time I am in a situation where I have the opportunity to testify, but feel fear - I am going to think of him!

As you are studying, you will likely have a lot of thoughts, insights, "ah-ha" moments, and inspiration that you should record. If there is not room on the page you are studying, just turn to the first available "My Commentary" page in the back of this journal and record your thoughts. These just may become the most valuable pages in your book!

In the left column, you can write the scripture you are studying and the page it is on so you can easily connect your commentary to the scripture.

You may only write a couple sentences or you may write for several pages!

* If you are struggling to know what to write, try asking yourself this question: "What doctrines and principles do I want my children and future posterity to see in this scripture and apply to their lives?"

Once you have written your commentary, go back to the original page and make a note on the bottom indicating that you have written commentary in the back of the book. For example, you could write "My Commentary on page 125".

ALMA 1 :1-15

THE BOOK OF ALMA		
WHAT IS THE SUBTITLE OF THIS BOOK?	WHAT DO YOU LEARN ABOUT THE AUTHOR OF THIS BOOK IN THE EXPLANATORY PARAGRAPH?	WHAT IS THE BOOK OF ALMA AN ACCOUNT OF? (SEE EXPLANATORY PARAGRAPH)

 KING MOSIAH   Record what you learn about King Mosiah in verse 1:

NEHOR   Doodle or record what you learn about Nehor in verses 2-6:

FALSE DOCTRINES   In the left column, make a list of false doctrines Nehor taught in verses 3-4. In the right column, correct the doctrine in your own words.

FALSE DOCTRINES	TRUTH

Doodle or explain what is happening in verses 5-6.

 **GIDEON**   What can you learn from Gideon and his example in verses 7-9?

IN EACH BOX, DRAW OR WRITE WHAT IS HAPPENING IN THESE VERSES. ALSO INCLUDE DOCTRINES, PRINCIPLES, PERSONAL INSIGHTS, AND LESSONS LEARNED.

10-11	12	13-14	15
	PRIESTCRAFT		

ALMA 1:16-33

IN EACH BOX, DOODLE OR RECORD A LESSON YOU CAN FIND IN EACH VERSE OR GROUP OF VERSES.

16	17-18	19-20

21-22	23-25	26-27

28-29	30-31	32-33

ALMA 2

1 Who is AMLICI, what do you learn about him, and what did he want? (verses 1–2)

2 What concerns did the people of the church have? (verses 3–4)

3 IN EACH BOX, DOODLE OR RECORD A LESSON YOU CAN FIND IN EACH VERSE OR GROUP OF VERSES.

The voice of the people	The "Amlicites"
5-7	8-11

War	War
12-15	16-19

The Amlicites & the Lamanites	"The Lord did hear their cries"
20-25	26-28

Alma vs. Amlici	King of Lamanites & his guards
29-31	32-33

Lamanites & Amlicites flee	Doodle your favorite phrase from this chapter:
34-38	

3

ALMA 3

Lessons Learned Study Alma 3 and then doodle or record three important lessons you learn from this chapter.

1

2

3

ALMA 4

IN EACH BOX, DOODLE OR RECORD WHAT IS HAPPENING AND A LESSON YOU CAN FIND IN EACH VERSE OR GROUP OF VERSES. AT THE BOTTOM OF EACH BOX, PICK ONE WORD THAT DESCRIBES THAT GROUP OF VERSES.

VERSES 1-5

WORD:

VERSES 6-8

WORD:

VERSES 9-10

WORD:

VERSES 11-14

WORD:

VERSES 15-18

WORD:

VERSES 19-20

WORD:

5

ALMA 5

Title for this chapter

Alma in Zarahemla

1 What do the italicized explanations just before the "Chapter 5" heading and verses 1 and 2 teach you about this chapter?

2 What events does Alma remind the people of in verses 3-5? | Why do you think Alma brings up these events?

3 This chapter is full of questions that Alma wanted the people to reflect upon. Find each question and record it in the first column. In the center column, record why you think Alma asked that question. In the right column, liken that question to yourself and record your own personal answers and insights.

TIP: VERSE 7 CAN HELP YOU ANSWER THESE QUESTIONS

QUESTION	WHY I THINK ALMA ASKED THAT QUESTION	MY PERSONAL ANSWERS / INSIGHTS
VERSE 6 1- Have you remembered the captivity of your fathers?		
2- Have you remembered his mercy & long suffering towards fathers?		
3- he delivered thour fathers from hell!		
VERSE 8 1- NOT DESTROYED!		
VERSE 9 1- Saved		
VERSE 10 1- on what conditions are they saved? 2- how did they have hope for salvation? 3- how did they escape death & chains of hell?		

6

	QUESTION	WHY I THINK ALMA ASKED THAT QUESTION	MY PERSONAL ANSWERS / INSIGHTS
VERSE 11 1-			
2-			
3-			
VERSE 14 1-			
2-			
3-			
VERSE 15 1-			
2-			
VERSE 16 1-			
VERSE 17 1-			

TIP: VERSES 12-13 CAN HELP YOU ANSWER THESE QUESTIONS

7

	QUESTION	WHY I THINK ALMA ASKED THAT QUESTION	MY PERSONAL ANSWERS / INSIGHTS
VERSE 18 1-			
VERSE 19 1-			
2-			
VERSE 20 1-			
VERSE 22 1-			
2-			
VERSE 23 1-			
VERSE 24 1-			
VERSE 26 1-			

TIP: VERSE 21 CAN HELP YOU ANSWER THIS QUESTION

TIP: VERSE 25 CAN HELP YOU ANSWER THIS QUESTION

	QUESTION	WHY I THINK ALMA ASKED THAT QUESTION	MY PERSONAL ANSWERS/ INSIGHTS
VERSE 27 1-			
2-			
3-			
VERSE 28 1-			
VERSE 29 1-			
VERSE 30 1-			

VERSES 31–36 What woes/warnings are given in verses 31–36?

VERSES 37–42 Pick 3 phrases that stand out to you in these verses. Doodle or write them in the left column, and then in the right column write about what that phrase teaches you.

PHRASE	WHAT EACH PHRASE TEACHES ME
1	
2	
3	

VERSES 43-52 What do the people learn about Alma in these verses? Make a list of everything you find.

	QUESTION	WHY I THINK ALMA ASKED THAT QUESTION	MY PERSONAL ANSWERS/ INSIGHTS
VERSE 53 1-			
2-			
3-			
VERSE 54 1-			
2-			
VERSE 55 1-			

TIP: VERSE 56 CAN HELP YOU ANSWER THIS QUESTION

VERSES 56-62 Pick 3 phrases that stand out to you in these verses. Doodle or write them in the left column, and then in the right column, write about what that phrase teaches you.

PHRASE	WHAT EACH PHRASE TEACHES ME
❶	
❷	
❸	

10

ALMA 6

Study this chapter, and fill the top part of this page with things you learn about the church in Zarahemla and about the city of Gideon.

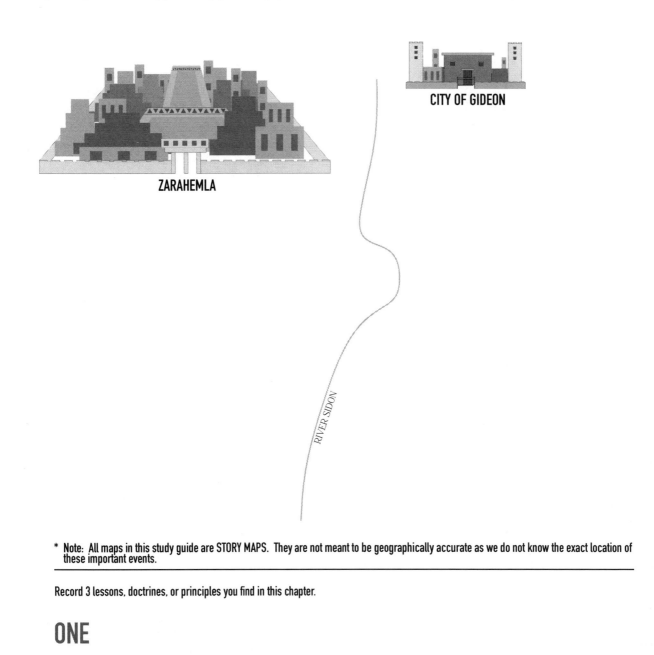

ZARAHEMLA

CITY OF GIDEON

RIVER SIDON

* Note: All maps in this study guide are STORY MAPS. They are not meant to be geographically accurate as we do not know the exact location of these important events.

Record 3 lessons, doctrines, or principles you find in this chapter.

ONE

- -

TWO

- -

THREE

11

ALMA 7

1 What does the italicized explanation just before the "Chapter 7" heading teach you about this chapter?

2 In each box doodle or record what is happening, doctrines and principles, or a lesson that stands out to you.

WHY THIS IS ALMA'S FIRST VISIT	WHAT ALMA HOPED TO FIND	WHAT ALMA HOPED TO FIND	THE MOST IMPORTANT THING TO COME
V. 1–2	V. 3–4	V. 5–6	V. 7
PREPARE FOR CHRIST	**PROPHECY OF CHRIST**	**PROPHECY OF CHRIST**	**PROPHECY OF CHRIST**
V. 8–9	V. 10	V. 11	V. 12
PROPHECY OF CHRIST	**BAPTISM / BEING BORN AGAIN**	**BAPTISM / BEING BORN AGAIN**	**PEOPLE OF GIDEON**
V. 13	V. 14	V. 15–16	V. 17–19
"NEITHER HATH HE A SHADOW OF TURNING"	**FATE OF THE FILTHY**	**AWAKE TO YOUR DUTY**	**REQUIRED CHRISTLIKE CHARACTERISTICS**
V. 20	V. 21	V. 22	V. 23
HOW TO HAVE GOOD WORKS IN YOUR LIFE	**BLESSINGS FOR THE SPOTLESS**	**ALMA'S SOURCE OF TESTIMONY**	**BLESSING TO PEOPLE OF GIDEON**
V. 24	V. 25	V. 26	V. 27

ALMA 8

Alma in Ammonihah

Doodle on this map what is happening in the verses given in the black boxes.

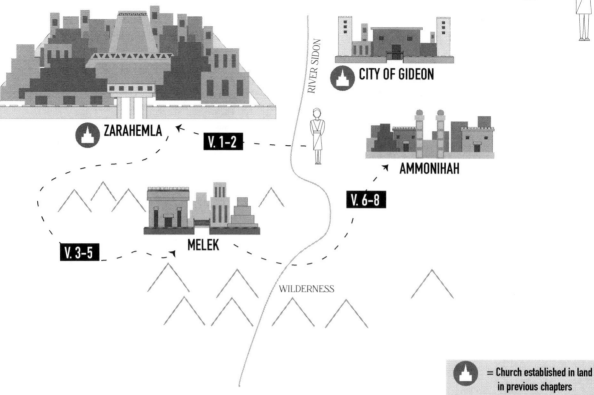

CITY OF GIDEON

ZARAHEMLA

V. 1-2

AMMONIHAH

V. 6-8

MELEK

V. 3-5

RIVER SIDON

WILDERNESS

= Church established in land in previous chapters

In each box doodle or record what is happening, doctrines and principles, or a lesson that stands out to you.

STATE OF THE PEOPLE IN AMMONIHAH	ALMA'S EFFORTS	PEOPLE'S RESPONSE TO ALMA	ANGEL
V. 9	V. 10	V. 11-13	V. 14-15

ANGEL	ALMA'S RESPONSE TO MESSAGE	AMULEK	ALMA AND AMULEK
V. 16-17	V. 18	V. 19-21	V. 22-26

ALMA AND AMULEK	ALMA AND AMULEK	LESSON LEARNED WHAT IS AN IMPORTANT LESSON THAT STANDS OUT TO YOU IN THIS CHAPTER?
V. 27-29	V. 30-32	

13

ALMA 9

<u>Title for this chapter</u>

Study each verse or group of verses. In the middle box, doodle or record what is happening: In the right box, record your thoughts, insights, and lessons learned.

VERSE	WHAT IS HAPPENING	THOUGHTS, INSIGHTS, & LESSONS LEARNED
1-3		
4-6		
7-10		
11-14		
15-17		
18-20		
21-23		
24-27		
28-30		
31-34		

ALMA 10 _____

AMULEK Doodle or write everything you learn about Amulek in verses 1-11

- -

Study each verse or group of verses. In the middle box, doodle or record what is happening. In the right box, record your thoughts, insights, and lessons learned.

VERSE	WHAT IS HAPPENING / BEING TAUGHT	THOUGHTS, INSIGHTS, & LESSONS LEARNED
12		
13-15		
16-17		
18-20		
21-23		
24-25		
26-27		
28-32		

ALMA 11

Amulek in Ammonihah

In each box, doodle or record what is happening, doctrines and principles, or a lesson that stands out to you.

WAGES FOR & RESPONSIBILITY OF JUDGES	JUDGE'S WAGE	NEPHITE COINAGE
V. 1-2	V. 3	V. 4

Nephite money is explained in verses 5-19. The following diagrams are to help you understand these verses. It is easiest to imagine the coins as equal to "weights and measures" to be used on a scale in order to weigh grain. The weights you see below can be stacked onto each other and are made of metal.

WEIGHTS   BARLEY   =   COINS

TIPS:
- EACH WEIGHT/METAL CUP EQUALED A SPECIFIC AMOUNT OF MONEY
- HOWEVER MANY WEIGHTS IT TOOK TO LEVEL OUT THE SCALE WOULD DETERMINE WHAT WAS OWED FOR THE GRAIN

1 Use this diagram to explain Alma 11:5, 8-10

GOLD

LIMNAH = SHUM + SEON + SENINE

$ = (coins)   SHUM $ = (coins)   SEON $ = (coins)   SENINE $

2 Use this diagram to explain Alma 11:7, 11-19

SILVER

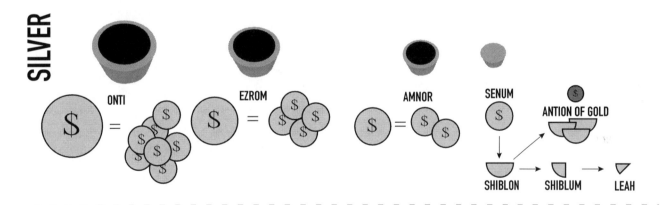

ONTI $ = (coins)   EZROM $ = (coins)   AMNOR $ = (coins)   SENUM $

ANTION OF GOLD

SHIBLON → SHIBLUM → LEAH

3 Using verses 7 and 15, write how much barley each value of coin could get you. Record the amount of barley under or by each coin above.

4 What were the judges doing in Ammonihah in order to receive more wages? (verse 20)

Throughout the remainder of this chapter, a man named Zeezrom questions Amulek. Under each verse, record what is happening, the question being asked, what is being taught, and/or the insights you find.

ALMA 10:31 AND 11:21 -

WHAT I LEARN ABOUT ZEEZROM:

QUESTION HE ASKED:

ALMA 11:22 -

ZEEZROM'S CHALLENGE:

ZEEZROM

ALMA 11:26 -

QUESTION HE ASKED:

ALMA 11:28 -

QUESTION HE ASKED:

ALMA 11:30 -

QUESTION HE ASKED:

ALMA 11:32 -

QUESTION HE ASKED:

ALMA 11:34 -

QUESTION HE ASKED:

ALMA 11:35 -

WHAT ZEEZROM TOLD THE PEOPLE:

ALMA 11:38 -

QUESTION HE ASKED:

ALMA 11:46 -

ZEEZROM'S REACTION:

ALMA 11:22 -

AMULEK'S ANSWER:

ALMA 11:23-25 -

AMULEK'S RESPONSE:

AMULEK

ALMA 11:27 -

AMULEK'S ANSWER:

ALMA 11:29 -

AMULEK'S ANSWER:

ALMA 11:31 -

AMULEK'S ANSWER:

ALMA 11:33 -

AMULEK'S ANSWER:

ALMA 11:34 -

AMULEK'S ANSWER:

ALMA 11:36-37 -

AMULEK'S ANSWER:

ALMA 11:39-45 -

DOCTRINE TAUGHT IN AMULEK'S ANSWER:

ALMA 12

Alma in Ammonihah

1 What can you learn from Alma in verses 1 and 2?

2 In each line, record a doctrine or principle that Alma taught.

Verse 3

Verse 4

Verse 5

Verse 6

Verse 7

ALMA

3 What impact did this have on Zeezrom in verse 8?

4 What question did Zeezrom ask Alma in verse 8?

5 In each line, record a doctrine or principle that Alma taught.

Verse 9

Verse 10

Verse 11

Verse 12

Verse 13

Verse 14

Verse 15

Verse 16

Verse 17

Verse 18

6 According to verse 19, what impact did Alma's words have on the people? Who then came forward in verse 20?

7 Study verses 20-37. In the left column below, record the two questions Antionah asked in verses 20-21. In the right column, record doctrine that Alma taught in response to those questions in verses 22-37.

QUESTIONS ASKED	DOCTRINES ALMA TAUGHT
QUESTION #1	
QUESTION #2	

ANTIONAH

ALMA 13

Alma in Ammonihah

This chapter contains teachings that Alma preached to the people of Ammonihah. In each box, record the doctrine and principles you can find in each verse.

THE LORD ORDAINS PRIESTS	WHEN PRIESTS ARE CALLED & PREPARED	WHO IS CALLED	WHAT THEY ARE CALLED TO DO
V. 1-2	V. 3	V. 4-5	V. 6

THE AGE OF THE PRIESTHOOD	HOW LONG THEY ARE HIGH PRIESTS	WHY THEY ARE CALLED	WASHED CLEAN
V. 7	V. 8-9	V. 10	V. 11-12

BRING FORTH REPENTANCE	MELCHIZEDEK	PURPOSE OF ORDINANCES	MELCHIZEDEK
V. 13	V. 14-15	V. 16	V. 17-18

MELCHIZEDEK	THE SCRIPTURES ARE BEFORE YOU	NOW IS THE TIME TO REPENT	IN PLAIN TERMS
V. 19	V. 20	V. 21-22	V. 23

THE LORD'S COMING IN GLORY	DO NOT PROCRASTINATE	CHRISTLIKE QUALITIES	SECOND DEATH
V. 24-26	V. 27	V. 28-29	V. 30-31

ALMA 14

Title for this chapter

Doodle on this illustration what is happening in the verses given in the black boxes. Include your insights and personal commentary.

SEARCHING SCRIPTURE
VERSE 1

CHIEF JUDGE

VERSES 14-17

ZEEZROM
VERSE 6

VERSES 2-5

VERSES 9-13

VERSE 7
ZEEZROM

VERSE 8

VERSES 18-25

VERSES 26-29

ALMA 15

_____
Title for this chapter

Doodle on this map what is happening in the verses given in the black boxes. Include your insights and personal commentary.

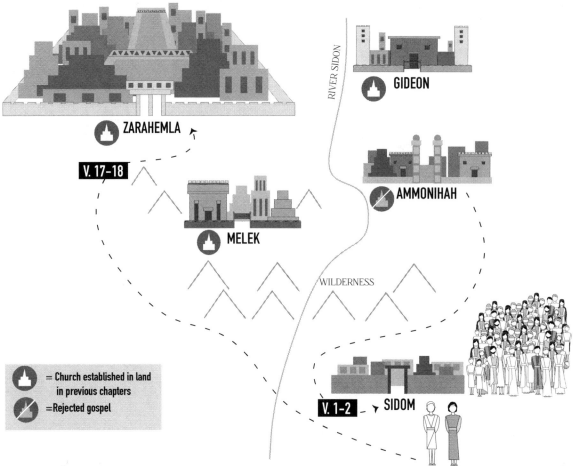

RIVER SIDON

GIDEON

ZARAHEMLA

V. 17-18

AMMONIHAH

MELEK

WILDERNESS

= Church established in land
   in previous chapters

=Rejected gospel

V. 1-2   SIDOM

Study each verse or group of verses. In the middle box, doodle or record what is happening. In the right box, record your thoughts, insights, and lessons learned.

VERSE(S)	WHAT IS HAPPENING / BEING TAUGHT	THOUGHTS, INSIGHTS, & LESSONS LEARNED
3		
4-5		
6-10		
11-12		
13-14		
15-16		
17-19		

ALMA 16

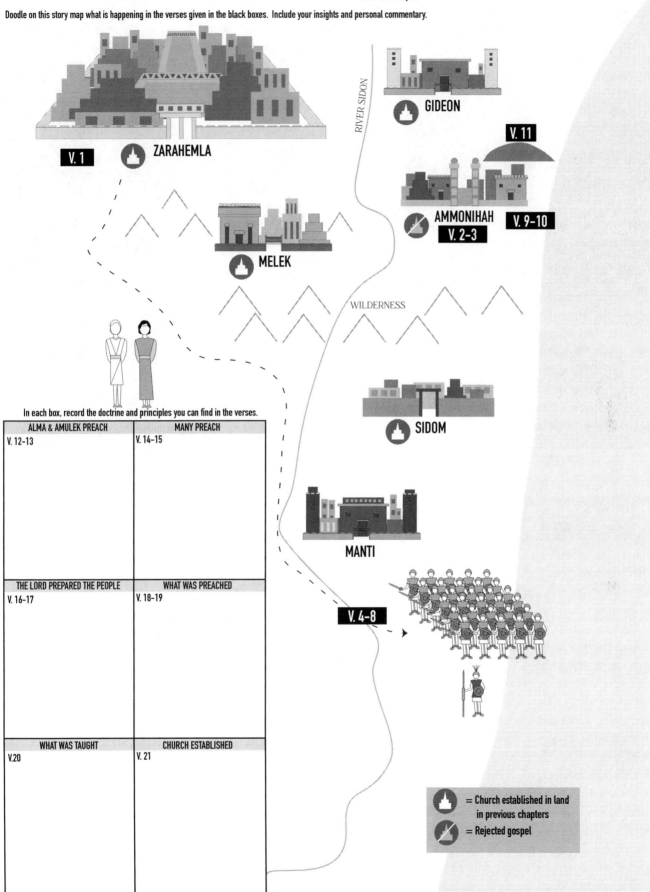

Doodle on this story map what is happening in the verses given in the black boxes. Include your insights and personal commentary.

ZARAHEMLA V. 1

GIDEON

MELEK

RIVER SIDON

AMMONIHAH V. 2-3
V. 11
V. 9-10

WILDERNESS

SIDOM

In each box, record the doctrine and principles you can find in the verses.

MANTI

V. 4-8

ALMA & AMULEK PREACH	MANY PREACH
V. 12-13	V. 14-15

THE LORD PREPARED THE PEOPLE	WHAT WAS PREACHED
V. 16-17	V. 18-19

WHAT WAS TAUGHT	CHURCH ESTABLISHED
V.20	V. 21

= Church established in land in previous chapters

= Rejected gospel

22

ALMA 17

1 What do you learn about Alma and the Sons of Mosiah in verses 1-5? Record what you find below:

ALMA

THE SONS OF MOSIAH

2 We now will learn what the Sons of Mosiah have been doing for the past 14 years while Alma was Chief Judge, High Priest, and preaching to the people. Doodle on this story map what is happening in the verses given in the black boxes. Include your insights and personal commentary.

V. 26-27

V. 33-38

V. 28-32

V. 25

ZARAHEMLA

V. 7-12

LAND OF ISHMAEL

V. 13-18

KING MOSIAH

SONS OF MOSIAH

KING LAMONI

V. 6

AMMON

V. 19-24

V. 39

2 LESSONS   What are 2 important lessons you can learn from this chapter? Record them in the boxes below.

ONE	TWO

ALMA 18

Title for this chapter

In each box, doodle or record what is happening, doctrines and principles, or a lesson that stands out to you.

KING LAMONI   AMMON

IS AMMON THE GREAT SPIRIT?	THE KING THINKS AMMON IS THE GREAT SPIRIT	LAMANITE BELIEFS / LAMONI'S CONCERN
V. 1-2	V. 3-4	V. 5-7

WHERE IS AMMON?	AMMON GOES TO KING	AMMON DISCERNS THOUGHTS OF KING	"I AM A MAN"
V. 8-10	V. 11-13	V. 14-16	V. 17-19

"BY WHAT POWER...?"	AMMON BEGINS TO TEACH	FAITH IN GOD	AMMON SPEAKS IN TERMS THE KING WOULD UNDERSTAND
V. 20-21	V. 22-23	V. 24-25	V. 26-27

THE CREATION	HEAVEN	CHILDREN OF GOD / THE HOLY GHOST	CREATION & FALL
V. 28-29	V. 30-32	V. 33-35	V. 36

HISTORY OF THE PEOPLE	PLAN OF SALVATION / COMING OF CHRIST	LAMONI BELIEVES	IMPACT ON LAMONI
V. 37-38	V. 39	V. 40-41	V. 42-43

24

ALMA 19

In each box, doodle or record what is happening, doctrines and principles, or a lesson that stands out to you.

	KING LAMONI	THE QUEEN CALLS FOR AMMON	WHAT WAS HAPPENING TO LAMONI
	V. 1	V. 2-5	V. 6
AMMON SEES KING	**THE QUEEN'S FAITH**	**LAMONI AWAKENS**	**LAMONI'S VISION**
V. 7-8	V. 9-10	V. 11-12	V. 13
AMMON OVERPOWERED WITH JOY	**ABISH**	**ABISH**	**LAMONI'S PEOPLE**
V. 14	V. 15-16	V. 17-18	V. 19-20
"WE SEE THAT AMMON COULD NOT BE SLAIN"	**WHO IS AMMON?**	**WHO IS AMMON?**	**ABISH AWAKENS QUEEN**
V. 21-23	V. 24-25	V. 26-27	V. 28-29
KING REBUKES HIS PEOPLE	**MANY WHO WOULD NOT HEAR**	**"AND THEY BECAME A RIGHTEOUS PEOPLE"**	**HIS ARM IS EXTENDED TO ALL PEOPLE**
V. 30-31	V. 32	V. 33-35	V. 36

ALMA 20 _____

1. Doodle on this story map what is happening in the verses 1-8. Include your insights and personal commentary.

2. In each box, doodle or record what is happening, doctrines and principles, or a lesson that stands out to you.

V. 9-10	V. 11-12
V. 13-14	V. 15-16
V. 17-18	V. 19-20
V. 21-22	V. 23-24

LAND OF ISHMAEL

V. 1
V. 2
V. 3
V. 4
V. 5

KING LAMONI

AMMON

V. 6-7

V. 8

LAND OF MIDDONI

= Church established in

= Rejected gospel

V. 25-26	V. 27	V. 28-29	V. 30

ALMA 21 _____

We now will learn what happened to Aaron while Ammon was in the Land of Ishmael. Doodle on this story map what is happening. Include your insights and personal commentary.

ZARAHEMLA

KING MOSIAH

SONS OF MOSIAH

ALMA 17:6

LAND OF ISHMAEL

ALMA 17:13-18

AMMON

KING LAMONI

ALMA 17:19-39

JERUSALEM

ALMA 21:1

LAND OF MIDDONI

ALMA 21:2-11

1- Who lived in Jerusalem? What were the people like there?

2- As Aaron began to preach unto the people, who rose to contend with him?

3- What are some questions this man asked Aaron in verse 5 and 6?

4- Fill in the blanks:

Amalekite: "We do believe that God will save _____ men."

Aaron: "Believest thou that the Son of God shall come to redeem mankind _____ their sins?

5- What is the difference between the two statements above?

6- Explain what happens in verses 8-10.

7- Read verses 11-14 and explain this picture.

8- Read verses 15-23. Continue to draw or write what happened after Aaron and others were delivered from prison.

ALMA 22 _____

1. Explain this picture after studying verses 1-3.

2. What questions did the king ask Aaron in verse 3?

3. How did Aaron take this opportunity to teach the King an important doctrine in verse 4?

4. What questions did the King ask Aaron in verses 5-6?

	WHAT AARON TAUGHT OR ASKED	WHAT THE KING SAID	INSIGHTS / LESSONS LEARNED
V. 7-8			
V.9			
V.10			
V.11			
V. 12			
V.13			
V.14			
V.15			
V.16			
V. 17-18			

19. Explain what happened in verses 19-27.

20. What do you learn about the land and how it was divided between the Nephites and the Lamanites in verses 27-34?

ALMA 23

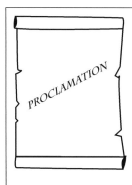

1. What did the king tell his people in the proclamation that was sent forth? (verses 1-4)

2. Explain this picture after you study verses 4-15.

3. What happened in verses 16-18?

4. What are some important lessons you can learn from this chapter?

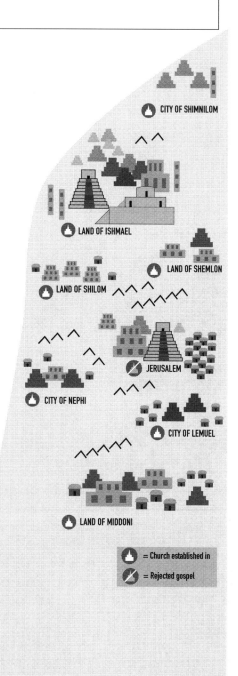

CITY OF SHIMNILOM

LAND OF ISHMAEL

LAND OF SHEMLON

LAND OF SHILOM

JERUSALEM

CITY OF NEPHI

CITY OF LEMUEL

LAND OF MIDDONI

= Church established in

= Rejected gospel

ALMA 24 _____

Title for this chapter

1. Doodle on this story map what is happening in the verses 1 and 2.

2. Explain this picture after studying verses 3 and 4.

TIP: ANTI-NEPHI-LEHI was a brother of LAMONI. It was not Lamoni. (See Index: "Anti-Nephi-Lehi".)

3. In your own words, explain what is happening in each verse or record an insight or lesson learned:

V. 5	
V. 6	
V. 7	
V. 8	
V. 9	
V. 10	
V. 11	
V. 12	
V. 13	
V. 14	
V. 15	
V. 16	
V. 17	
V. 18	
V. 19	
V. 20	
V. 21	
V. 22	
V. 23	
V. 24	
V. 25	
V. 26	
V. 27	
V. 28	
V. 29	
V. 30	

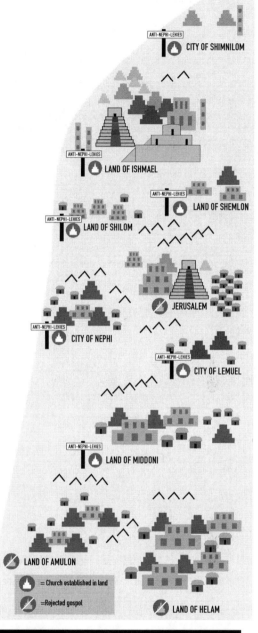

FAVORITE PHRASE

What is your favorite phrase from this chapter?

ALMA 25

In your own words, explain what is happening in each verse or record an insight or lesson learned:

V. 1	
V. 2	
V. 3	
V. 4	
V. 5	
V. 6	
V. 7	
V. 8	
V. 9	
V. 10	
V. 11	
V. 12	
V. 13	
V. 14	
V. 15	
V. 16	
V. 17	

FAVORITE PHRASE

What is your favorite phrase from this chapter?

ALMA 26

In each box, doodle or record what is happening, doctrines and principles, or a lesson that stands out to you.

ALMA 26

AMMON

"COULD WE HAVE SUPPOSED?"	"WE HAVE BEEN INSTRUMENTS"	IMAGERY: THE HARVEST
V. 1-2	V. 3-4	V. 5

IMAGERY: THE HARVEST	"IF WE HAD NOT COME UP..."	"I WILL REJOICE IN MY GOD"	"IN HIS STRENGTH I CAN DO ALL THINGS"
V. 6-7	V. 8-9	V. 10-11	V. 12

BROUGHT INTO HIS EVERLASTING LIGHT	WHO CAN GLORY TOO MUCH IN THE LORD?	"REMEMBER WHAT WE USED TO BE LIKE?"	WHO KNOWS GOD'S MYSTERIES
V. 13-15	V. 16-17	V. 18-20	V. 21-22

REMEMBER WHEN...	REMEMBER WHEN...	THEIR INTENT	SUFFERINGS
V. 23-24	V. 25	V. 26	V. 27-28

EXPERIENCES THEY HAD	THE FRUITS OF THEIR LABORS	LEVEL OF CONVERSION	GOD IS MINDFUL OF EVERY PEOPLE
V. 29-30	V. 31-32	V. 33-34	V. 35-37

ALMA 27

Title for this chapter

Study each set of verses and then, in each box, record a phrase, insight, or a lesson that stood out to you.

VERSES 1–4	VERSES 5–8

VERSES 9–12	VERSES 13–19

VERSES 20–24	VERSES 25–30

ALMA 28

_____

Title for this chapter

1. Doodle or write on this story map what you learned in Alma 27.

2. Add to this map what happened in Alma 28:1-6.

3. What important 3 principles did you find in verses 7-14?

1

2

3

RIVER SIDON

ZARAHEMLA

GIDEON

MELEK

AMMONIHAH

ANTI-NEPHI-LEHIES CITY OF SHIMNILOM

ANTI-NEPHI-LEHIES LAND OF ISHMAEL

ANTI-NEPHI-LEHIES LAND OF SHEMLON

WILDERNESS

ANTI-NEPHI-LEHIES LAND OF SHILOM

SIDOM

JERUSALEM

LAND OF BOUNTIFUL

ANTI-NEPHI-LEHIES CITY OF NEPHI

ANTI-NEPHI-LEHIES CITY OF LEMUEL

MANTI

JERSHON

ANTI-NEPHI-LEHIES LAND OF MIDDONI

LAND OF AMULON

= Church established in land

=Rejected gospel

SEA

LAND OF HELAM

34

ALMA 29

Study each set of verses, and then in each box, record what you learn about Alma, a phrase, insight, or a lesson that stood out to you.

VERSES 1–2	VERSES 3–5

ALMA

VERSES 6–8	VERSES 9–11

VERSES 12–15	VERSES 16–17

ALMA 30 _____

Title for this chapter

This chapter is about Korihor, the antichrist. In each box, record the doctrine and principles you can find in each verse.

AFTER THE WAR	AN ANTI-CHRIST	THE LAW	KORIHOR
V. 1-5	V. 6 **KORIHOR**	V. 7-11	V. 12-14
"YE CANNOT KNOW"	**EFFECT OF KORIHOR'S TEACHINGS**	**PEOPLE OF AMMON**	**KORIHOR TAKEN BEFORE GIDDONAH**
V. 15-17	V. 18	V. 19-20	V. 21-23
KORIHOR: "YE SAY... I SAY"	**KORIHOR: THERE IS NO GOD**	**KORIHOR TAKEN BEFORE ALMA**	**KORIHOR ACCUSES ALMA**
V. 24-26	V. 27-28	V. 29-30 **ALMA**	V. 31-34
ALMA QUESTIONS KORIHOR	**ALMA: "WHAT EVIDENCE HAVE YE?"**	**ALMA: "I HAVE ALL THINGS AS A TESTIMONY"**	**KORIHOR: "SHOW ME A SIGN"**
V. 35-38 ALMA - - - - - - - - - - KORIHOR	V. 39-40	V. 41-42	V. 43-44 KORIHOR - - - - - - - - - - ALMA
ALMA: "WILL YE DENY?"	**THE SIGN**	**THE CURSE**	**AND THUS WE SEE**
V. 45-48 ALMA - - - - - - - - - - KORIHOR	V. 49-53	V. 54-57	V. 58-60

ALMA 31

1. Doodle on this story map what is happening in the verses 1 –7.

2. Consider this missionary force that Alma took with him to the Zoramites. What kind of experience, knowledge, and background did this group bring with them?

ALMA AARON OMNER HIMNI ZEEZROM AMULEK SHIBLON CORIANTON

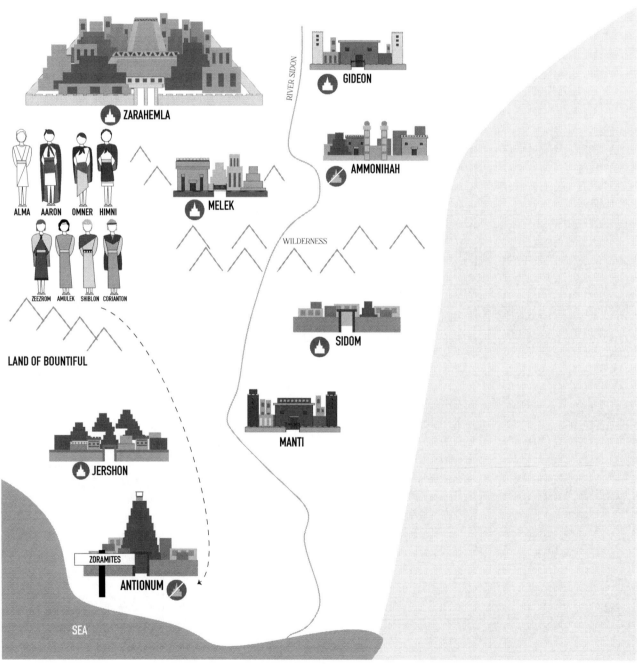

1. What do you learn about the Zoramites in verses 1, 2, and 8–11?

2. What did Alma and the others find as they arrived? (v. 12–14)

3. The Zoramites' prayer is outlined in verses 15–18. In the left column, record the parts of their prayer that are TRUE DOCTRINE. In the right column, record the FALSE DOCTRINE.

TRUE	FALSE

4. What is happening, and what lessons can you learn in verses 19–25?

5. What stands out to you in Alma's prayer in verses 26–35?

6. As Alma and the others separated to go preach to the people, what lessons can you learn in verses 36–38?

ALMA 32 _____
Title for this chapter

ALMA

As you study this chapter, follow the template below and record what you find in each group of verses: In the first column, doodle or record what is happening or being taught. In the middle column, record your own thoughts and insights. In the last column, write ONE phrase that explains an important lesson you learned in those verses.

VERSES	WHAT IS HAPPENING OR BEING TAUGHT	MY THOUGHTS AND INSIGHTS	ONE PHRASE
V. 1-3			
V. 4-7			
V. 8-12			
V. 13-15			
V. 16-19			
V. 20-25			
V. 26-27			
V. 28-30			
V. 31-32			
V. 33-35			
V. 36-40			
V. 41-43			

39

ALMA 33

ALMA

As you study this chapter, follow the template below and record what you find in each group of verses: In the first column, doodle or record what is happening or being taught. In the middle column, record your own thoughts and insights. In the last column, write ONE PHRASE or doodle a PICTURE that explains an important lesson you learned in those verses.

Title for this chapter

VERSES	WHAT IS HAPPENING OR BEING TAUGHT	MY THOUGHTS AND INSIGHTS	ONE PHRASE OR PICTURE
V. 1			
V. 2-3			
V. 4-8			
V. 9-11			
V. 12-14			
V. 15-16			
V. 17-18			
V. 19-20			
V. 21-23			

AMULEK

ALMA 34 _____

This chapter contains teachings that Amulek preached to the Zoramites. In each box, record the doctrine and principles you can find in each verse.

YOU HAVE BEEN TAUGHT OF CHRIST	THE GREAT QUESTION	ALMA QUOTED OTHER PROPHETS	AMULEK ADDS HIS TESTIMONY
V. 1-2	V. 3-5	V. 6-7	V. 8

IF THERE WERE NO ATONEMENT	AN INFINITE AND ETERNAL SACRIFICE	WHAT THE LAW REQUIRES	FULFILLMENT OF LAW OF MOSES
V. 9	V. 10	V. 11-12	V. 13-14

THE INTENT OF THE LAST SACRIFICE	CRY...	PRAY CONTINUALLY	CHARITY
V. 15-16	V. 17-25	V. 26-27	V. 28-29

NOW IS THE TIME	DO NOT PROCRASTINATE	YE CANNOT SAY THIS	THE LORD DWELLETH NOT IN UNHOLY TEMPLES
V. 30-31	V. 32-33	V. 34-35	V. 36

WORK OUT YOUR SALVATION	TAKE UPON THE NAME OF CHRIST	BE WATCHFUL UNTO PRAYER	HAVE PATIENCE
V. 37	V. 38	V. 39	V. 40-41

ALMA 35

Study each set of verses, and then in each box, record a phrase, insight, or a lesson that stood out to you. If an illustration is given, explain what it means.

VERSES 1-2	VERSES 3-6

JERSHON

ALMA AARON OMNER HIMNI ZEEZROM AMULEK SHIBLON CORIANTON

ZORAMITES

ANTIONUM

VERSES 7-9	VERSES 10-12

VERSES 13-14	VERSES 15-16

ALMA 36

TIP: Alma 36–42 contain the words of Alma to his sons Helaman, Shiblon and Corianton. Alma 36–37 are specifically to Helaman, Alma 38 is to Shiblon, and Alma 39–42 are to Corianton.

ALMA 36

ALMA   HELAMAN

REMEMBER...	A PROMISE	HOW ALMA KNOWS
V. 1–2	V. 3	V. 4–5

ALMA'S CONVERSION	ALMA'S CONVERSION	ALMA'S CONVERSION	ALMA'S CONVERSION / GODLY SORROW
V. 6–7	V. 8–9	V. 10–11	V. 12

ALMA'S CONVERSION / GODLY SORROW	ALMA'S CONVERSION / GODLY SORROW	ALMA'S CONVERSION / GODLY SORROW	ALMA'S CONVERSION / GODLY SORROW
V. 13	V. 14	V. 15	V. 16

ALMA TURNS TO CHRIST	JOY REPLACES SUFFERING	ALMA'S VISION	BORN OF GOD
V. 17–18	V. 19–21	V. 22	V. 23–24

OTHERS KNOW AS HE KNOWS	ALMA'S PAST EXPERIENCES & FUTURE ONES	ALWAYS REMEMBER THIS	A PROMISE
V. 25–26	V. 27–28	V. 29	V. 30

ALMA 37

In each box, doodle or record what is happening, doctrines and principles, or a lesson that stands out to you.

ALMA 37

ALMA   **HELAMAN**

RECORD KEEPER	PLATES OF BRASS	SMALL AND SIMPLE THINGS
V. 1-2	V. 3-5	V. 6-7

THE POWER OF SCRIPTURE	THE POWER OF SCRIPTURE	FOR A WISE PURPOSE	REMEMBER THESE THINGS
V. 8	V. 9-10	V. 11-12	V. 13-14

WARNING	PROMISE	THE LORD FULFILLS HIS PROMISES	24 PLATES / HISTORY OF THE JAREDITES
V. 15	V. 16-17	V. 18-20	V. 21-22

HISTORY OF THE JAREDITES	THEIR SECRET OATHS MUST BE KEPT FROM THE PEOPLE	THE WICKEDNESS OF THE JAREDITES	WHAT HELAMAN SHOULD TEACH THE PEOPLE
V. 23-27	V. 28-29	V. 30-31	V. 32-34

WHAT HELAMAN SHOULD DO	THE LIAHONA	THE EASINESS OF THE WAY	LOOK TO GOD AND LIVE
V. 35-37	V. 38-42	V. 43-46	V. 47

ALMA 38

Title for this chapter

As you study chapter 38, doodle or record the things you learn in each box below.

WHAT I LEARN ABOUT SHIBLON	COUNSEL ALMA GIVES SHIBLON

ALMA 38

FAVORITE PHRASES AND TEACHINGS IN THIS CHAPTER	INSIGHTS AND LESSONS I LEARNED FROM THIS CHAPTER

ALMA   SHIBLON

ALMA 39 _____

ALMA TO CORIANTON

As you study this chapter, follow the template below and record what you find in each group of verses: In the first column, doodle or record what is happening or being taught. In the middle column, record your own thoughts and insights. In the last column, write ONE PHRASE or doodle a PICTURE that explains an important lesson you learned in those verses.

	WHAT IS HAPPENING OR BEING TAUGHT	MY THOUGHTS AND INSIGHTS	ONE PHRASE/PICTURE
V. 1-2			
V. 3-4			
V. 5-6			
V. 7			
V. 8			
V. 9			
V. 10-11			
V. 12-13			
V. 14			
V. 15-16			
V. 17			
V. 18-19			

ALMA 40

As you study this chapter, follow the template below and record what you find in each group of verses: In the first column, doodle or record what is happening or being taught. In the middle column, record your own thoughts and insights. In the last column, write ONE PHRASE or doodle a PICTURE that explains an important lesson you learned in those verses.

	WHAT IS HAPPENING OR BEING TAUGHT	MY THOUGHTS AND INSIGHTS	ONE PHRASE/PICTURE
V. 1–2			
V. 3–4			
V. 5–6			
V. 7			
V. 8–10			
V. 11–12			
V. 13–14			
V. 15–16			
V. 17–18			
V. 19–21			
V. 22–24			
V. 25–26			

ALMA 41

Title for this chapter

ALMA TO CORIANTON

As you study this chapter, follow the template below and record what you find in each group of verses: In the first column, doodle or record what is happening or being taught. In the middle column, record your own thoughts and insights. In the last column, write ONE PHRASE or doodle a PICTURE that explains an important lesson you learned in those verses.

	WHAT IS HAPPENING OR BEING TAUGHT	MY THOUGHTS AND INSIGHTS	ONE PHRASE/PICTURE
V. 1			
V. 2-3			
V. 4			
V. 5			
V. 6-7			
V. 8			
V. 9			
V. 10			
V. 11			
V. 12-13			
V. 14			
V. 15			

ALMA 42 _____

ALMA TO CORIANTON

As you study this chapter, follow the template below and record what you find in each group of verses: In the first column, doodle or record what is happening or being taught. In the middle column, record your own thoughts and insights. In the last column, write ONE PHRASE or doodle a PICTURE that explains an important lesson you learned in those verses.

	WHAT IS HAPPENING OR BEING TAUGHT	MY THOUGHTS AND INSIGHTS	ONE PHRASE/PICTURE
V. 1			
V. 2-3			
V. 4-5			
V. 6-7			
V. 8-9			
V. 10-11			
V. 12-13			
V. 14-15			
V. 16-22			
V. 23-25			
V. 26-28			
V. 29-31			

ALMA 43 _____

1. Doodle on this story map what is happening in verses 1-16.

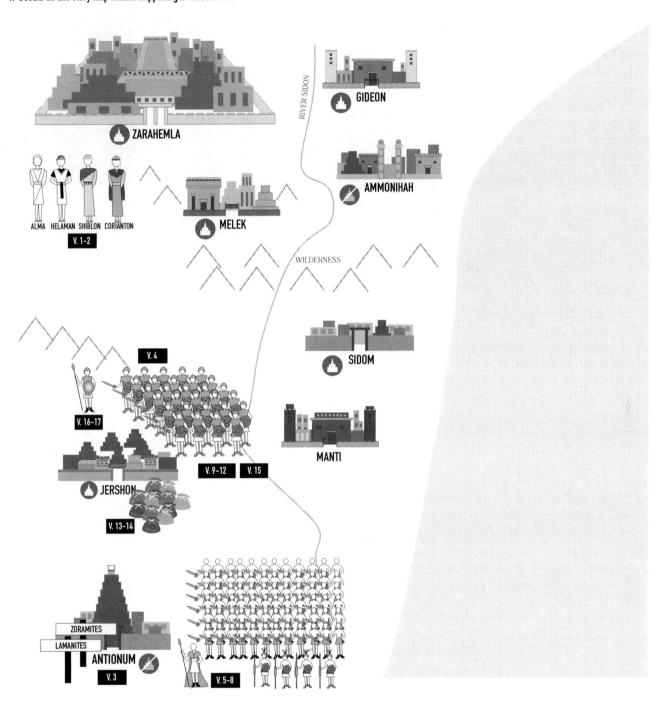

2. In your own words, explain what is happening in each verse, or record an insight or lesson learned:

V. 17-21	
V. 22	
V. 23-24	

V. 25–26	
V. 27–28	
V. 29–33	
V. 34–36	
V. 37–38	
V. 39–40	
V. 41–42	
V. 43–44	
V. 45	
V. 46–47	
V. 48–49	
V. 50	
V. 51–53	
V. 54	

How can you liken the PHYSICAL battle in this chapter to the SPIRITUAL battle we face?

ALMA 44 _____

In your own words, explain what is happening in each verse, or record an insight or lesson learned:

MORONI   ZERAHEMNAH

V. 1-2	
V. 3	
V.4	
V. 5	
V. 6-7	
V. 8-9	
V. 10-11	
V. 12	
V. 13-14	
V. 15	
V. 16	
V. 17	
V. 18-19	
V. 20	
V. 21	
V. 22	
V. 23-24	

ALMA 45

Study each set of verses and then in each box, record what is happening, a phrase, insight, or a lesson that stood out to you.

NEPHITES REJOICE	ALMA QUESTIONS HELAMAN		
V. 1	V. 2-8  ALMA HELAMAN	QUESTIONS	ANSWERS

ALMA INSTRUCTS HELAMAN	ALMA PROPHESIES: FUTURE OF NEPHITES	ALMA PROPHESIES: NEPHITES BECOME EXTINCT	ALMA PROPHESIES: NEPHITES BECOME EXTINCT
V. 9	V. 10	V. 11	V. 12

ALMA PROPHESIES: NO MORE NEPHITES	ALMA PROPHESIES: NEPHITES BECOME LAMANITES	ALMA BLESSES SONS & LAND	ALMA CURSES LAND
V. 13	V. 14	V. 15	V. 16

ALMA BLESSES CHURCH	ALMA'S DEATH	ALMA TRANSLATED	HELAMAN PREACHES
V. 17	V. 18	V. 19	V. 20

WORD OF GOD WAS NEEDED	CHURCH BUSINESS THROUGHOUT LAND	DISSENSIONS ARISE	PRIDE
V. 21	V. 22	V. 23	V. 24

ALMA 46 _____

Study each set of verses and then in each box, record what is happening, a phrase, insight, or a lesson that stood out to you.

V. 1-7	V. 8-10	V. 11-13
HELAMAN AMALICKIAH	AND THUS WE SEE...	

V. 14-18	V. 19-21	V. 22
		THE COVENANT

V. 23-27	V. 28-35	V. 36-41

54

ALMA 47

Title for this chapter

Study each set of verses and then in each box, record what is happening, a phrase, insight, or a lesson that stood out to you.

V. 1-4	V. 5-7	V. 8
AMALICKIAH	KING	AMALICKIAH'S INTENTION:

V. 9-12	V. 13	V. 14-19
	THE DEAL:	

V. 20-30	V. 31-35	V. 36

What life lessons can you find in this chapter?

ALMA 48 _____

In your own words, explain what is happening in each verse or record an insight or lesson learned:

V. 1–2	
V. 3	
V.4	
V. 5–6	
V. 7	
V. 8–9	
V. 10	
V. 11	
V. 12	
V. 13	
V. 14–15	
V. 16	
V. 17	
V. 18–19	
V. 20–21	
V. 22–23	
V. 24–25	

ALMA 49 _____
Title for this chapter

As you study this chapter, follow the template below and record what you find in each group of verses: In the middle box, doodle or record what is happening or being taught. In the far right box, record your own thoughts and insights.

VERSES	WHAT IS HAPPENING OR BEING TAUGHT	LIFE LESSONS
V. 1–3	AMMONIHAH	
V. 4–5		
V. 6–7		
V. 8–9		
V. 10–11		
V. 12–13	NOAH	
V. 14–15		
V. 16–17		
V. 18–20		
V. 21–24		
V. 25–27		
V. 28–30		

ALMA 50

Title for this chapter

MAKE A LIST
VERSES 1-12

of everything Moroni did to prepare the Nephites for attacks from the Lamanites.

LIKEN
How can you liken these verses to your own life and protect yourself from attacks from sin and temptation?

Doodle on this story map what is happening in verses 13–17 and 25–40.

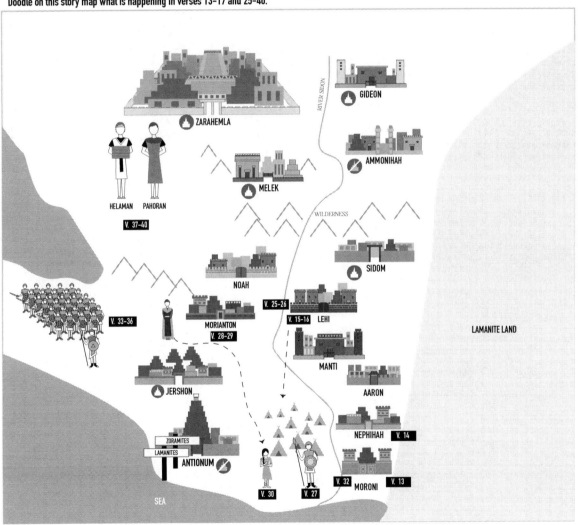

What important principles do you learn in verses 17–24?

ALMA 51 _____

Title for this chapter

In each box, record the doctrines and principles you can find in the verses.

CONTENTION CONCERNING LAWS	KING-MEN	FREEMEN	VOICE OF THE PEOPLE
V. 1–3	V. 4–5	V. 6	V. 7

PAHORAN

THOSE IN FAVOR OF KINGS	A CRITICAL TIME	REFUSAL OF KING-MEN	A PETITION
V. 8	V. 9–12	V. 13	V. 14–16

KING-MEN PRIDE PULLED DOWN	END TO KING-MEN	MEANWHILE THE LAMANITES...	CITY OF MORONI "NOT SUFFICIENTLY STRONG"
V. 17–20	V. 21	V. 22	V. 23

Doodle on this story map what is happening in verses 24-37.

ZARAHEMLA

RIVER SIDON

GIDEON

AMMONIHAH

MELEK

WILDERNESS

V. 28-37

NOAH

SIDOM

BOUNTIFUL

MORIANTON

LEHI

LAMANITE LAND

MANTI

JERSHON

AARON

GID

NEPHIHAH V. 24-25

ZORAMITES

MULEK

LAMANITES

V. 26-27

ANTIONUM

MORONI

SEA

OMNER

59

ALMA 52

In each box, doodle or record what is happening, doctrines and principles, or a lesson that stands out to you.

LAMANITES FRIGHTENED	AMMORON	TEANCUM'S PLAN	MORONI SENDS REINFORCEMENTS & ORDERS
V. 1-2	V. 3-4	V. 5-6	V. 7-11

DANGEROUS CIRCUMSTANCES	TAKING BACK THE CITY OF MULEK	WAITING FOR MORONI & MAKING A PLAN	TRY #1
V. 12-14	V. 15-17	V. 18-19	V. 20

TRY #2	CITY OF MULEK TAKEN BACK	LAMANITE ARMY IN PURSUIT OF TEANCUM	WHAT MORONI TOLD HIS ARMY TO DO
V. 21-25	V. 26	V. 27-31	V. 32

BATTLE	ATTACK FROM THE BACK	GIVE UP WEAPONS OF WAR	PRISONERS
V. 33-35	V. 36	V. 37-38	V. 39-40

WHAT ARE SOME LIFE LESSONS YOU CAN LEARN IN THIS CHAPTER?

ALMA 53

In each box, doodle or record what is happening, doctrines and principles, or a lesson that stands out to you.

PRISONERS	LEHI	PRISONER ORDERS	STRONGHOLDS
V. 1	V. 2	V. 3-4	V. 5-6

PREPARATIONS & FORTIFICATIONS	MEANWHILE...	PEOPLE OF AMMON	ABOUT TO BREAK OATH
V. 7	V. 8-9	V. 10-13	V. 14

HELAMAN'S CONCERN	THEIR SONS	THE SONS' COVENANT	2,000 SONS
V. 15	V. 16	V. 17	V. 18

WANTED HELAMAN FOR A LEADER	THE SONS	THE SONS	2,000 STRIPLING WARRIORS
V. 19	V. 20	V. 21	V. 22-23

WHAT ARE SOME LIFE LESSONS YOU CAN LEARN IN THIS CHAPTER?

ALMA 54  _____

In this space, explain what is happening in verses 1–4.

As you read the letters, record points that stand out to you and any lessons you learn as you study them.

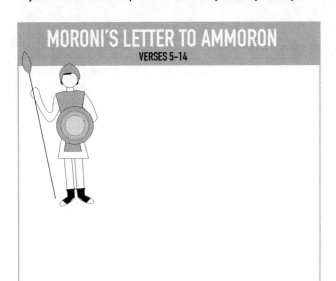

MORONI'S LETTER TO AMMORON
VERSES 5–14

AMMORON'S LETTER TO MORONI
VERSES 15–24

ALMA 55 _____

Title for this chapter

1. What was Moroni's reaction to Ammoron's letter? **VERSES 1-3**

2. Describe what Moroni did in order to take back the City of Gid from the Lamanites. **VERSES 4-24**

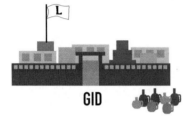

GID

3. What important points and lessons can you find in **VERSES 25-35** ?

STORY MAP : ALMA 56-62

As you study chapters 56–62 (using the following pages) use this story map to visualize what happened. Add your own lines, arrows, descriptions, and drawings to the map.

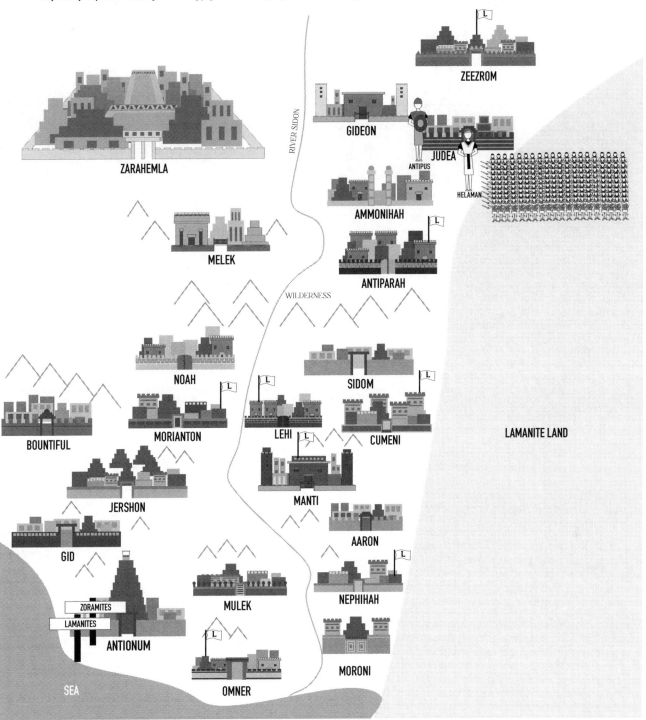

WHAT ARE SOME LIFE LESSONS YOU CAN LEARN IN THESE CHAPTERS?

ALMA 56

Title for this chapter

As you study this chapter, follow the template below and record what you find in each group of verses: In the first box, doodle or record what is happening or being taught. In the far right box, record ONE LIFE LESSON you can find in those verses.

	WHAT IS HAPPENING, DOCTRINES & PRINCIPLES TAUGHT	LIFE LESSON
V. 1-8		
V. 9-14		
V. 15-20	TIP: ANTIPUS IS A NEPHITE COMMANDER	
V. 21-26		
V. 27-29		
V. 30-33	STRATEGIC MANEUVER	
V. 34-38		
V. 39-42		
V. 43-46		
V. 47-48		
V. 49-54		
V. 55-57		

ALMA 57

As you study this chapter, follow the template below and record what you find in each group of verses: In the first box, doodle or record what is happening or being taught. In the far right box, record ONE LIFE LESSON you can find in those verses.

HELAMAN → MORONI

	WHAT IS HAPPENING, DOCTRINES & PRINCIPLES TAUGHT	LIFE LESSON
V. 1-5		
V. 6-8		
V. 9-12		
V. 13-15		
V. 16-18		
V. 19-21		
V. 22-23		
V. 24-25		
V. 26-27		
V. 28-30		
V. 31-33		
V. 34-36		

ALMA 58

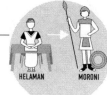

Title for this chapter

As you study this chapter, follow the template below and record what you find in each group of verses: In the first box, doodle or record what is happening or being taught. In the far right box, record ONE LIFE LESSON you can find in those verses.

	WHAT IS HAPPENING, DOCTRINES & PRINCIPLES TAUGHT	LIFE LESSON
V. 1-3		
V. 4-6		
V. 7-9		
V. 10-11		
V. 12-13		
V. 14-17		
V. 18-21		
V. 22-25		
V. 26-29		
V. 30-33		
V. 34-38		
V. 39-41		

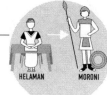

HELAMAN

MORONI

ALMA 59

As you study the verses below, doodle or write about WHAT IS HAPPENING, a FAVORITE PHRASE, a LESSON LEARNED, or DOCTRINES & PRINCIPLES you find.

V. 1-3	V. 4
V. 5-6	V. 7-8
V. 9	V. 10
V. 11-12	V. 13

WHAT ARE SOME LIFE LESSONS YOU CAN LEARN IN THIS CHAPTER?

ALMA 60

MORONI → PAHORAN

Title for this chapter

Study Moroni's letter to Pahoran and, in your scriptures, mark your favorite phrases that Moroni uses. When you are finished, choose 10 of your favorite phrases and record them (and the verses you found them in) below. Include your thoughts about each phrase in the space to the right.

1 PHRASE: VERSE: THOUGHTS & INSIGHTS:

2 PHRASE: VERSE: THOUGHTS & INSIGHTS:

3 PHRASE: VERSE: THOUGHTS & INSIGHTS:

4 PHRASE: VERSE: THOUGHTS & INSIGHTS:

5 PHRASE: VERSE: THOUGHTS & INSIGHTS:

6 PHRASE: VERSE: THOUGHTS & INSIGHTS:

7 PHRASE: VERSE: THOUGHTS & INSIGHTS:

8 PHRASE: VERSE: THOUGHTS & INSIGHTS:

9 PHRASE: VERSE: THOUGHTS & INSIGHTS:

10 PHRASE: VERSE: THOUGHTS & INSIGHTS:

ALMA 61

MORONI   PAHORAN

Study each set of verses, and then in each box, doodle what Parhoran explained was happening, a phrase, insight, or a lesson that stood out to you.

VERSES 1-4	VERSES 5-8

VERSES 9-10	VERSES 11-14

VERSES 15-18	VERSES 19-21

_____
Title for this chapter

In each box, doodle or record what is happening, doctrines and principles, or a lesson that stands out to you.

MORONI'S REACTION TO PAHORAN'S LETTER	MORONI'S MARCH	MORONI & PAHORAN UNITE FORCES	TRIALS OF KING-MEN
V. 1-2	V. 3-5	V. 6-8	V. 9-11

MORONI SENDS ARMIES TO HELAMAN, LEHI, & TEANCUM	MORONI & PAHORAN SEEK TO REGAIN NEPHIHAH	MORONI'S PLAN	HOW THEY REGAINED NEPHIHAH
V. 12-13	V. 14-18	V. 19-21	V. 22-26

DESIRE OF LAMANITE PRISONERS	MORONI TAKES ARMY TO LAND OF LEHI	LAMANITE ARMY ALL GATHERED IN ONE PLACE	TEANCUM
V. 27-29	V. 30-32	V. 33-34	V. 35-37

LAMANITES DRIVEN OUT OF LAND	WHY THE NEPHITES WERE SPARED	SOME HARDENED, SOME SOFTENED	MORONI & HELAMAN RETURN HOME
V. 38-39	V. 40	V. 41	V. 42-43
			MORONIHAH

HELAMAN & BRETHREN PREACH TO THE PEOPLE	CHURCHES AND JUDGES SET IN PLACE	PEOPLE WERE NOT PRIDEFUL	PEOPLE REMEMBERED AND PRAYED
V. 44-45	V. 46-47	V. 48-49	V. 50-52

ALMA 63

Study each set of verses, and then in each box, doodle what is happening, doctrines and principles, or a lesson that stands out to you.

VERSES 1-3	VERSES 4-6
SHIBLON	

VERSES 7-9	VERSES 10-13
	HELAMAN (JR.)

VERSES 14-15	VERSES 16-17

72

HELAMAN 1

Title for this chapter

TIP: A powerful lesson we can learn from the first six chapters of Helaman is that righteous men and women can operate in a world filled with secret combinations, corrupt governments, and Satan's manipulative powers.

Study each group of scriptures, and explain what is happening in each picture. Add additional doodles, pictures, thoughts, and lessons learned to the pictures below.

VERSES 1-4

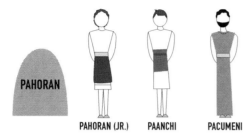

PAHORAN

PAHORAN (JR.)   PAANCHI   PACUMENI

VERSES 5-8

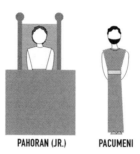

PAHORAN (JR.)   PACUMENI

PAANCHI

VERSES 9-12

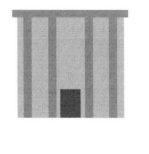

VERSES 13-21

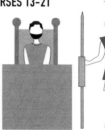

PACUMENI   CORIANTUMR

TUBALOTH

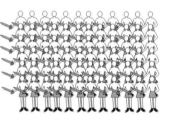

VERSES 22-32

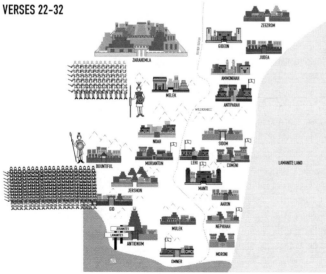

VERSES 33-34

ZARAHEMLA

HELAMAN 2

As you study this chapter, follow the template below and record what you find in each group of verses. In the 2nd column, doodle or record what is happening and the doctrines and principles being taught. In the last column, record your own thoughts and insights.

VERSES	WHAT IS HAPPENING, DOCTRINES & PRINCIPLES TAUGHT	MY THOUGHTS AND INSIGHTS
V. 1-2	HELAMAN (JR.)	
V. 3-4	KISHKUMEN / GADIANTON	
V. 5		
V. 6-7	SERVANT OF HELAMAN	
V. 8		
V. 9		
V. 10		
V. 11		
V. 12		
V. 13-14	MORMON'S COMMENTARY — TIP: Mormon has one thousand years of Nephite history available to him and he says this!	

HELAMAN 3

_____

Title for this chapter

In each box, doodle or record what is happening, doctrines and principles, or a lesson that stands out to you.

NO CONTENTION	MANY LEAVE	DESOLATE	BUILD HOUSES OF CEMENT
V. 1-2	V. 3-4	V. 5-6	V. 7-8

SCARCE TIMBER	MANY RECORDS KEPT	A HUNDREDTH PART	MANY RECORDS OF EVERY KIND
V. 9-11	V. 12-13	V. 14	V. 15-16

GREAT CONTENTIONS	HELAMAN JUDGES RIGHTEOUSLY	HELAMAN'S TWO SONS	SECRET COMBINATIONS
V. 17-19	V. 20	V. 21	V. 22-23

PROSPERITY IN CHURCH	THUS WE MAY SEE...	YEA, THUS WE SEE...	YEA, WE SEE
V. 24-26	V. 27	V. 28	V. 29-30

REJOICING, JOY, PEACE	PERSECUTION OF RIGHTEOUS	GROWING PRIDE	NEPHI
V. 31-33	V. 34-35	V. 36	V. 37

75

HELAMAN 4

Study each set of verses, and then in each box, doodle what was happening, a phrase, an insight, or a lesson that stood out to you. At the bottom of each box, come up with a phrase that explains the set of verses.

VERSES 1-3	VERSES 4-8

PHRASE:

PHRASE:

VERSES 9-13	VERSES 14-17

PHRASE:

PHRASE:

VERSES 18-23	VERSES 24-26

PHRASE:

PHRASE:

HELAMAN 5

In each box, doodle or record what is happening, doctrines and principles, or a lesson that stands out to you.

CEZORAM	MORE WHO CHOSE EVIL THAN GOOD	NEPHI & LEHI PREACH	WHAT HELAMAN HAD TAUGHT HIS SONS
V. 1	V. 2-3	V. 4-5	V. 6-7

WHAT HELAMAN HAD TAUGHT HIS SONS	WHAT HELAMAN HAD TAUGHT HIS SONS	WHAT HELAMAN HAD TAUGHT HIS SONS	NEPHI & LEHI REMEMBER & TEACH
V. 8-9	V. 10-11	V. 12-13	V. 14-16

NEPHI & LEHI PREACH WITH POWER	NEPHI & LEHI CAST INTO PRISON	STANDING IN THE MIDST OF FIRE	NEPHI & LEHI SPEAK
V. 17-19	V. 20-22	V. 23-25	V. 26

EARTH SHOOK	THERE CAME A VOICE	THE VOICE SPEAKS AGAIN	THE FACES OF ANGELS
V. 27-28	V. 29-31	V. 32-33	V. 34-37

AMINADAB	A PILLAR OF FIRE	HOLY SPIRIT	300 SOULS
V. 38-41	V. 42-44	V. 45-47	V. 48-52

HELAMAN 6 _____

Title for this chapter

While you are studying each group of verses, doodle or record what is happening during each year below. Include any lessons you learn as you study.

62ⁿᵈ / 63ᴿᴰ YEAR
V. 1-6

64ᵀᴴ YEAR
V. 7-13

65ᵀᴴ YEAR
V. 14

66ᵀᴴ YEAR
V. 15

67ᵀᴴ YEAR
V. 16-32

68ᵀᴴ YEAR
V. 33-41

THE CONDITION OF THE PEOPLE OF NEPHI
VERSES 1-6

Study verses 1-6, and record in this box what was happening among the Nephites at this time.

NEPHI'S WORDS

Study verses 7-29 in your scriptures, marking the teachings and phrases that stand out to you. After you have studied those verses, choose five phrases or teachings that stand out to you and write about them below. In the left column, record the teaching or phrase. In the second column, record the verse it is found in. In the last column, record your thoughts about that phrase and why is stands out to you.

TEACHING / PHRASE	VERSE	THOUGHTS / INSIGHTS

HELAMAN 8

Study each group of verses below. Once you have studied the verses, ponder them and then decide on ONE important principle or life lesson in those verses, and write or doodle about it in the boxes below.

VERSES 1-6

VERSES 7-10

VERSES 11-15

VERSES 16-20

VERSES 21-24

VERSES 25-28

HELAMAN 9

As you study this chapter, follow the template below and record what you find in each group of verses: In the first column, doodle or record what is happening or being taught. In the far right column, record your own thoughts and insights.

VERSES	WHAT IS HAPPENING, DOCTRINES & PRINCIPLES TAUGHT	MY THOUGHTS AND INSIGHTS
V. 1-2		
V. 3-5		
V. 6-9		
V. 10-15		
V. 16-18		
V. 19-20		
V. 21-24	NEPHI'S REBUKE	
V. 25-36	NEPHI GIVES ANOTHER SIGN	
V. 37-38		
V. 39-41		

WHAT ARE SOME LIFE LESSONS YOU CAN LEARN FROM THIS CHAPTER?

HELAMAN 10

Study this chapter, and fill the page with REASONS WE SHOULD listen to and follow the Lord's servants. You can doodle or write about PROMISES Nephi received from the Lord, GIFTS Nephi had, or THINGS NEPHI DID.

NEPHI

HELAMAN 11 _____

While you are studying each group of verses, doodle or record what is happening during each year below. Include any lessons you learn as you study.

73RD YEAR
V. 1-5

_____

74th YEAR
V. 5

_____

75th YEAR
V. 6-16

_____

76th YEAR
V. 17-21

_____

77th YEAR
V. 21

_____

78th YEAR
V. 22

_____

79th YEAR
V. 23

_____

80th YEAR
V. 24-29

_____

81st YEAR
V. 30-35

_____

82nd YEAR
V. 36

_____

83rd YEAR
V. 36

_____

84th YEAR
V. 36

_____

85th YEAR
V. 37-38

HELAMAN 12 _____

Title for this chapter

MORMON'S TEACHINGS

In this chapter, Mormon stops telling us the story of the Nephites and gives us some of his insights. Mormon's insights are very valuable because he has all of the Nephite history in front of him and knows what is coming to the Nephite nation. He can see what choices and actions are leading to inevitable consequences. Study Helaman 12 in your scriptures, and mark the phrases that stand out to you. When you are finished studying the chapter, pick five phrases or teachings and write about them in the boxes below. In the left column, record the teaching or phrase. In the second column, record the verse or verses it is found in. In the last column, record your own thoughts and insights.

TEACHING / PHRASE	VERSE	THOUGHTS / INSIGHTS

84

HELAMAN 13 _____

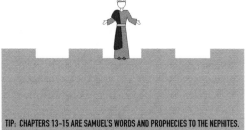

Title for this chapter

1. WHAT DO YOU LEARN ABOUT THE LAMANITES IN VERSE 1?

2. WHAT DO YOU LEARN ABOUT SAMUEL IN VERSES 2-4?

TIP: CHAPTERS 13-15 ARE SAMUEL'S WORDS AND PROPHECIES TO THE NEPHITES.

In each box below, record something Samuel taught the Nephites.

V. 5	V. 6	V. 7	V. 8-9
V. 10	V. 11-12	V. 13-14	V. 15-17
V. 18-19	V. 20-21	V. 22	V. 23-24
V. 25-26	V. 27-28	V. 29-30	V. 31
V. 32-33	V. 34-35	V. 36-37	V. 38-39

HELAMAN 14 _____

Title for this chapter

In each box below, record or draw something Samuel taught the Nephites.

V. 1-2	V. 3	V. 4	V. 5
V. 6-7	V. 8-9	V. 10	V. 11
V. 12-13	V. 14-15	V. 16-17	V. 18
V. 19	V. 20	V. 21-22	V. 23-25
V. 26-27	V. 28-29	V. 30	V. 31

WHAT IS ONE IMPORTANT LESSON TAUGHT IN THIS CHAPTER?

HELAMAN 15 _____

Title for this chapter

In each box below, record or draw something Samuel taught the Nephites.

V. 1–2	V. 3	V. 4	V. 5
V. 6	V. 7	V. 8	V. 9
V. 10	V. 11	V. 12	V. 13
V. 14	V. 15	V. 16	V. 17

WHAT IS ONE IMPORTANT LESSON TAUGHT IN THIS CHAPTER?

HELAMAN 16 _____

While you are studying each group of verses, doodle or record what is happening during each year below. Include any lessons you learn as you study.

TIP: This chapter covers the five years before Christ was born in Bethlehem. These verses show the state of the Nephites on the other side of the world just before Christ was born.

86th YEAR
V. 1-9

87th YEAR
V. 10

88th YEAR
V. 11

89th YEAR
V. 12

90th YEAR
V. 13-25

3 NEPHI 1

LEHI

NEPHI

ALMA

ALMA
THE YOUNGER

HELAMAN

HELAMAN (JR.)

NEPHI

NEPHI (JR.)

Title for this chapter

1. Read the description under the title "Third Nephi" and verses 1–3 in your scriptures, and then explain the illustration down the left side of the page.

2. What does this quote by President Benson teach you about the importance of 3 Nephi?

"The record of the Nephite history just prior to the Savior's visit reveals many parallels to our own day as we anticipate the Savior's second coming. The Nephite civilization had reached great heights. They were prosperous and industrious. They had built many cities with great highways connecting them. They engaged in shipping and trade. They built temples and palaces. Mormon noted that the Nephites 'did not sin ignorantly, for they knew the will of God concerning them' (3 Nephi 6:18).

"...what a blessing it would be if every family would read together 3 Nephi, discuss its sacred contents, and then determine how they can liken it unto themselves and apply its teachings in their lives.

President Ezra Taft Benson
April 1987 General Conference

In each box below, record or doodle what is happening or something you learn in the following scriptures in 3 Nephi 1.

V. 1–3	V. 4	V. 5–6	V. 7–8
V. 9	V. 10–12	V. 13–14	V. 15
V. 16–18	V. 19–20	V. 21	V. 22–23
V. 24–25	V. 26–27	V. 28–29	V. 30

3 NEPHI 2

While you are studying each group of verses, doodle or record what is happening during each year below. Include any lessons you learn as you study.

TIP: During this time, Christ was growing up in Israel.

95th-99th YEAR
V. 1-4

A.D. 9
V. 5-8

TIP: When the new star appeared in the sky, the Nephites changed how they reckoned their time. Instead of marking the years from when they put their first judge in place, they kept track of time from when the star had appeared. It had now been 9 years, and is therefore A.D. 9 or the ninth year.

A.D. 10, 11, [12]
V. 9-10

A.D. 13
V. 11-16

A.D. 14
V. 17

A.D. 15
V. 18-19

3 NEPHI 3 _____

Title for this chapter

1. What happened in verses 1 and 2?

GIDDIANHI   LACHONEUS

2. In your scriptures, draw a line above verse 2 and another line below verse 10. In between those two lines is the letter from Giddianhi. Read his letter, and in your scriptures, mark all of the things he says that stand out to you. In the space below, write about four things that Giddianhi says or does to try to make Lachoneus feel like there is no alternative other than to give in to his demands.

1	
2	
3	
4	

3. Pick one of the four things you wrote about above and liken it unto how Satan tries to use the same tactics on us.

4. Study verses 11-17. Mark all of the things that Lachoneus did to not be swayed by Giddianhi and to prepare the people against an attack of any kind. In the space below, write about four things that Lachoneus did.

1	
2	
3	
4	

5. Study verses 18-21 and answer the following questions:

- Who is Gidgiddoni and what do you learn about him?

- What did Gidgiddoni do to lead the people?

GIDGIDDONI

6. Study verses 22-26. In the space below, record what the Nephites did to prepare themselves against the robbers.

What can we learn from the Nephites in this chapter? How can we apply some of these same principles to our lives?

3 NEPHI 4

In each box, doodle or record what is happening, doctrines and principles, or a lesson that stands out to you.

ROBBERS COME TO BATTLE	NO FOOD	NEPHITES IN ONE BODY	ROBBERS FORCED TO BATTLE
V. 1	V. 2-3	V. 4	V. 5-6

APPEARANCE OF ARMY	NEPHITE ARMIES PRAY	NEPHITE ARMIES PREPARED	NEPHITE VICTORY
V. 7	V. 8	V. 9-10	V. 11-12

GIDDIANHI DIES	NEW TACTIC TO OVERCOME NEPHITES	ZEMNARIHAH / ROBBERS TRY AGAIN	ADVANTAGE TO NEPHITES
V. 13-14	V. 15-16	V. 17	V. 18-19

ROBBERS HAD LITTLE PROVISIONS	ROBBERS WITHDRAW	NEPHITES CUT THEM OFF	PRISONERS TAKEN
V. 20-21	V. 22-23	V. 24-26	V. 27

DEATH OF ZEMNARIHAH	NEPHITE CRY	SINGING AND PRAISING	NEPHITES HAD BEEN DELIVERED
V. 28	V. 29-30	V. 31-32	V. 33

3 NEPHI 5

TIP: During this time, Christ is a young man. Luke 3:23 states that Christ was about thirty years of age when He began His ministry. So, He would be soon approaching that momentous time.

A.D. 22-25

Study these verses, and then doodle or record what is happening during each year below. Include any lessons you learn as you study.

VERSES 1-7

VERSES 8-26

Mormon, who is telling us this story, stops the record and gives us His powerful testimony. Take some time to study verses 8-26 and ponder his words. Pick 3 things he said (or things you learned while studying these verses) and write about them below.

ONE

TWO

THREE

3 NEPHI 6

In your own words, explain what is happening in each verse or group of verses, or record an insight or lesson learned:

V. 1–2	
V. 3–4	
V. 5–6	
V. 7–9	
V. 10–11	
V. 12	
V. 13	
V. 14	
V. 15–16	
V. 17–18	
V. 19–20	
V. 21–22	
V. 23–24	
V. 25–26	
V. 27–28	
V. 29	
V. 30	

3 NEPHI 7 _____
Title for this chapter

Study each set of verses, and then in each box, doodle what was happening, a phrase, an insight, or a lesson that stood out to you. At the bottom of each box, come up with a phrase that explains the set of verses or a life lesson you learned in those verses.

VERSES 1-4	VERSES 5-8

PHRASE: | PHRASE:

VERSES 9-10	VERSES 11-12

PHRASE: | PHRASE:

VERSES 13-14	VERSES 15-16

PHRASE: | PHRASE:

VERSES 17-18	VERSES 19-20

PHRASE: | PHRASE:

VERSES 21-22	VERSES 23-26

PHRASE: | PHRASE:

3 NEPHI 8 _____

Title for this chapter

Study 3 Nephi 8, use this story map to visualize what happened. Add your own drawings, descriptions, etc. to illustrate what happened to the cities.

In each box, explain in one sentence what happened in each group of verses.

V. 1–4	V. 5–12	V. 13–19	V. 20–23	V. 24–25

3 NEPHI 9

1. Following all of the destruction, what happens in verse 1?

2. What important things does the voice of Christ teach the people in verse 2?

3. Study verses 3–11, and write all over the story map below what Christ says about the destruction of the cities. Add descriptions, draw pictures, make notes, etc.

In each box below, record at least one doctrine or principle taught in each verse. Include any thoughts or insights you have.

V. 12–13	V. 14	V. 15–16
V. 17	V. 18	V. 19
V. 20	V. 21	V. 22

3 NEPHI 10 _____

Title for this chapter

VERSES 1-2

Ponder these verses and imagine what this moment might have been like for those who experienced it. Doodle or record your thoughts here.

VERSES 3-7

Study these verses and consider this question: WHAT MESSAGE DOES THE LORD WANT THEM TO RECEIVE? Record your thoughts here.

* TIP: NOTE HOW CHRIST USED "HAVE I," "WOULD I," AND "WILL I" IN VERSES 4, 5 AND 6.

VERSES 8-11

Write or doodle one significant thing that happened in each of these scriptures.

VERSE 8	VERSE 9	VERSE 10	VERSE 11

VERSES 12-13

Doodle or record what you learn about those who were saved.

VERSES 14-17

Imagine you were asked to give a talk in church about these verses. What would you title your talk? What principles would you talk about?

TITLE:

PRINCIPLES:

VERSES 18-19

What is Mormon telling us in these verses? How do you think Mormon felt as he recorded these words?

3 NEPHI 11

Title for this chapter

VERSES 1-2
What specific things do you think they may have been showing each other and talking about?

THE VOICE
Record everything you learn about THE VOICE in the verses below.

VERSE 3
VERSE 4
VERSE 5
VERSE 6
VERSE 7

VERSE 8
Study this verse and find a doctrine or principle that stands out to you. Write about it in this space.

THE INTRODUCTION
Study VERSES 8-11 and notice how Christ introduced Himself. What are some things that stand out to you about His introduction?

VERSE 12
How is verse 12 different than verse 8? What lessons can you learn as you compare these two verses?

ONE BY ONE
Study VERSES 13-17 and imagine being able to interview someone who was there that day. What might they share about this experience?

How do you think Nephi felt in this moment?

BAPTISM

VERSES 21-41

After Christ takes the time to introduce Himself and spends time with the people, He addresses the important topic of BAPTISM. Why do you think He addressed this so quickly after His appearance?

Study each verse or group of verses and record what you learn about Baptism.

VERSES 21-23
VERSES 24-26
VERSES 27-28
VERSES 29-30
VERSES 31-32
VERSES 33-34
VERSES 35-36
VERSES 37-38

THIS IS MY DOCTRINE

VERSES 39-41

Doodle, diagram, or write about what these verses teach you about the importance of Christ's doctrine.

3 NEPHI 12 _____

Title for this chapter

TIP

Chapters 12 and 13 contain a life-changing sermon Christ gave to the Nephites. He gives them instruction on how to receive the blessings of the Gospel. You can compare these chapters to Matthew 5 and 6, for it is similar to the Sermon on the Mount where Christ gave the Beatitudes to the Jews. Study these chapters and ask yourself, "If Christ came, which of these teachings would He give to us today?"

V. 1-2   INSTRUCTION TO THE MULTITUDE OF PEOPLE

Study these scriptures and doodle or write about specific things Christ told the multitude.

BEATITUDES

Christ teaches about essential traits that we must gain in order to become like Him. In the April 1977 General Conference, Elder Royden G. Derrick said this: "Each of the Beatitudes represents a specific step in our orderly progression towards perfection and teaches us how to qualify ourselves for exaltation."

In the chart below write or doodle about each beatitude.

VERSES	WHAT CHRIST TELLS US TO "BE"	TIP	HOW HAVING THIS CHARACTERISTIC WOULD IMPACT YOUR LIFE AND THE LIVES OF THOSE AROUND YOU	PERSONAL GOALS
3		"What is meant by 'poor in spirit'? Is it not humility, which renders us teachable and eager to learn? They who feel themselves spiritually poor approach God, asking him to supply their needs. They ... learn his laws and try diligently to obey him. " - Elder O. Leslie Stone, Oct. 1974 General Conference		
4		"We should always remember the Lord intended that we should have problems to meet and solve as a part of our training in this life to help us prepare for the next phase of our eternal existence." - Elder O. Leslie Stone, Oct. 1974 General Conference		
5		"The meek are those who are gentle, kind, patient, tolerant; not proud, mighty, or conceited. In Proverbs we read, 'He that is slow to anger is better than the mighty.'(Prov. 16:32.) "Meekness must not, however, be confused with self-depreciation. Because it involves self-control, it is not a weak, but a heroic quality." - Elder O. Leslie Stone, Oct. 1974 General Conference		
6		"Those who seek after truth shall be fed in rich abundance.... "If we really hunger and thirst after righteousness, then it is our duty to know and to do the will of him who sent us here." - Elder O. Leslie Stone, Oct. 1974 General Conference		
7		"They that show mercy shall receive mercy. "Someone made this compassionate statement: 'There is no better exercise for the heart than to reach down and lift someone up.'" - Elder O. Leslie Stone, Oct. 1974 General Conference		
8		"If we strive to be like God, then we will do all we possibly can to cast from our minds and actions all unholy and ungodly things, that our motives will be honorable and our hearts pure." - Elder O. Leslie Stone, Oct. 1974 General Conference		
9		"Peacemakers are those who try to save themselves and their fellows from strife. Our Heavenly Father delights in peace, and all who seek to bring about peace shall be like God... and shall be called the children of God. "The Lord has commanded us to love all men, including our enemies. He expects us to be peacemakers.... It is better to turn the other cheek, to go the extra mile, to give our coat... than to offend." - Elder O. Leslie Stone, Oct. 1974 General Conference		
10-12		"Today members of the Church do not often face persecution in the form of physical violence or harm, but perhaps some application can be made to the pressures we may feel from society, particularly the peer group pressures that our young people feel when they live up to the standards of dress and morality set by our present-day leaders. If these young people are prayerful and live the commandments, they will feel good about these high standards and will be able to stand up to criticism." - Elder O. Leslie Stone, Oct. 1974 General Conference		

WHO YOU ARE

Study verses 13-16, and write or doodle what Christ teaches us about who we are and what our role is.

V. 13-16

[blank box]

OLD vs. NEW LAW

TIP

On Mount Sinai God gave Moses a law for the children of Israel to live. This law was known as "The Law of Moses". It was meant to be a temporary or "lesser" law to help prepare the people for a higher law with higher blessings. Over time, the Law of Moses was central to Jewish life and it was a criminal offense to break it. To many Jews there could not be a higher law than the Law of Moses and invited great opposition as Christ taught of a higher law when He ministered to the Jews in the flesh. Just as Christ taught of the higher law to the Jews, in this chapter, He is teaching the same law to the Nephites. We, who have the fulness of the Gospel of Jesus Christ, should be doing all we can to live this higher law.

VS. 17-20

This scripture comes right before Christ gives the higher law. What do these scriptures teach you?

[blank box]

Below, study each old and new law.

VERSES	OLD LAW	NEW LAW	PERSONAL GOALS
21-26		TIP: "Raca" is a derogatory or mocking term that expresses contempt or derision.	
27-32			
33-37			
38-42			
43-44			

VS. 45-48

These verses teach you about the PURPOSE of the higher law. Doodle or write about what you learn in these verses.

[blank box]

TIP

"'Be ye therefore perfect, even as your Father which is in heaven is perfect.'"
"Keeping this commandment can be a concern because each of us is far from perfect, both spiritually and temporally....
"Mortal perfection can be achieved as we try to perform every duty, keep every law, and strive to be as perfect in our sphere as our Heavenly Father is in his. If we do the best we can, the Lord will bless us according to our deeds and the desires of our hearts.
"But Jesus asked for more than mortal perfection. The moment he uttered the words "even as your Father which is in heaven is perfect," he raised our sights beyond the bounds of mortality. Our Heavenly Father has eternal perfection. This very fact merits a much broader perspective.
"In Matt. 5:48, the term perfect was translated from the Greek teleios, which means 'complete....' The infinitive form of the verb is teleiono, which means 'to reach a distant end, to be fully developed, to consummate, or to finish.' Please note that the word does not imply 'freedom from error'; it implies 'achieving a distant objective....'
"The perfection that the Savior envisions for us is much more than errorless performance. It is the eternal expectation as expressed by the Lord in his great intercessory prayer to his Father—that we might be made perfect and able to dwell with them in the eternities ahead."

Elder Russell M. Nelson, October 1995 General Conference

3 NEPHI 13 _____

Title for this chapter

In this chapter, Christ gives specific counsel about some important topics. In the spaces below, doodle or write about what you learn about each topic. At the bottom of each box, come up with a single phrase that encompasses what you learned about that topic.

SERVICE
V. 1-4

PHRASE:

PRAYER
V. 5-13

PHRASE:

FORGIVENESS
V. 14-15

PHRASE:

FASTING
V. 16-18

PHRASE:

TREASURES
V. 19-21

PHRASE:

TWO MASTERS
V. 22-24

PHRASE:

INSTRUCTION TO THE TWELVE
V. 25-34 At this point, Christ turns to the Twelve He had chosen and gives them specific instructions. Study these verses and then doodle or write about the instructions Christ gave to them.

3 NEPHI 14 _____

Title for this chapter

In this chapter, Christ gives specific counsel about some important topics. In the spaces below, doodle or write about what you learn about each topic. At the bottom of each box, come up with a single phrase that encompasses what you learned about that topic.

JUDGING OTHERS

V. 1-5

PHRASE:

ASK

V. 6-11

PHRASE:

"GOLDEN RULE"

V. 12

PHRASE:

STRAIT & NARROW

V. 13-14

PHRASE:

HOW TO KNOW A FALSE PROPHET

V. 15-20

PHRASE:

WISE & FOOLISH

V. 21-27

PHRASE:

3 NEPHI 15

As you study this chapter, follow the template below and record what you find in each group of verses: In the first column, doodle or record what is happening and the doctrines and principles being taught. In the second column, record your own thoughts and insights. In the last column, come up with ONE PHRASE or DRAW A PICTURE that portrays an important teaching in those verses.

VERSES	WHAT IS HAPPENING, DOCTRINES & PRINCIPLES TAUGHT	MY THOUGHTS AND INSIGHTS	ONE PHRASE/PICTURE
V. 1			
V. 2			
V. 3-4			
V. 5-7			
V. 8-9			
V. 10			
V. 11-13			
V. 14-16			
V. 17-18			
V. 19-20			
V. 21-22			
V. 23-24			

3 NEPHI 16 _____
Title for this chapter

OTHER SHEEP v. 1-3

What do you learn in these verses about other followers of Christ around the world?

A COMMAND v. 4-5

What specific command did Christ give?

Study verses 6-20 and look for everything you learn about the GENTILES and about the HOUSE OF ISRAEL. Write down everything you learn about the Gentiles in the left column and everything you learn about the House of Israel in the right column.

GENTILES

HOUSE OF ISRAEL

3 NEPHI 17 _____

Study each set of verses, and then in each box, record or draw what was happening. You can also write about a doctrine or principle, or record a phrase or a lesson that stands out to you. At the bottom of each box, come up with a life lesson you can learn from those verses.

VERSES 1-2	VERSE 3
LIFE LESSON:	LIFE LESSON:

VERSE 4	VERSES 5-6
LIFE LESSON:	LIFE LESSON:

VERSES 7-8	VERSES 9-10
LIFE LESSON:	LIFE LESSON:

VERSES 11-12	VERSES 13-15
LIFE LESSON:	LIFE LESSON:

VERSES 16-17	VERSES 18-20
LIFE LESSON:	LIFE LESSON:

VERSES 21-23	VERSES 24-25
LIFE LESSON:	LIFE LESSON:

3 NEPHI 18 _____
Title for this chapter

THE SACRAMENT · VERSES 1-14

Doodle or record what you learn about THE SACRAMENT in these verses.

Study the following groups of verses, and after you study the verses, pick ONE PHRASE or TEACHING that stands out to you about each topic. Doodle each phrase and write about what it teaches you in each box below.

PRAYING ALWAYS
VERSES 15-21

FELLOWSHIPPING OTHERS
VERSES 22-25

DANGER OF PARTAKING OF SACRAMENT UNWORTHILY
VERSES 26-29

HOW TO TREAT THOSE WHO ARE IN NEED OF REPENTANCE
VERSES 30-34

DISCIPLES GIVEN POWER
VERSES 35-37

JESUS ASCENDS INTO HEAVEN
VERSES 38-39

3 NEPHI 19 _____

VERSES 1-3

What great lessons can you learn from these verses?

Using verse 4, label the twelve disciples below. Also, study verses 4-9, and record some important principles you find about the twelve disciples.

We can learn a lot about PRAYER and HOW TO IMPROVE OUR PRAYERS in verses 10-36. Study those verses, and mark things that stand out to you. Ponder what you have marked, and then doodle or record 6 lessons you learn about prayer.

ONE

TWO

THREE

FOUR

FIVE

SIX

3 NEPHI 20 _____

Title for this chapter

As you study this chapter, follow the template below and record what you find in each group of verses: In the first column, doodle or record what is happening and the doctrines and principles being taught. In the second column, record your own thoughts and insights. In the last column, come up with ONE PHRASE or DRAW A PICTURE that portrays an important teaching in those verses.

VERSES	WHAT IS HAPPENING, DOCTRINES & PRINCIPLES TAUGHT	MY THOUGHTS AND INSIGHTS	ONE PHRASE/PICTURE
V. 1			
V. 2-8			
V. 9-10			
V. 11-14			
V. 15-17			
V. 18-21			
V. 22-24			
V. 25-28			
V. 29-34			
V. 35-39			
V. 40-43			
V. 44-46			

3 NEPHI 21

Doodle or write about important principles or teachings you find in the groups of verses below. At the end of each box, write one thing that summarizes what you learned in those verses.

VERSES 1-4

VERSES 5-8

VERSES 9-10

VERSES 11-22

VERSES 23-25

VERSES 26-29

3 NEPHI 22-23 _____

Title for these chapters

In chapter 22, Christ quotes Isaiah who taught about Zion in the last days and about Israel being gathered.   Study these chapters, and find 3 phrases that teach you something about ZION or the GATHERING OF ISRAEL. Doodle those phrases below, and write about what they teach you.

3 NEPHI 22: CHRIST QUOTES ISAIAH

ONE

TWO

THREE

In chapter 23, Christ approves the words of Isaiah and commands us to search the prophets. Study each group of verses below, and doodle or write about what those verses teach you.

23:1-3	23:4-5	23:6-8	23:9-11	23:12-14

3 NEPHI 24-25

As you study these chapters, follow the template below and record what you find in each group of verses: In the first column, doodle or record what is happening and the doctrines and principles being taught. In the second column, record your own thoughts and insights. In the last column, come up with ONE PHRASE or DRAW A PICTURE that portrays an important teaching in those verses.

VERSES	WHAT IS HAPPENING, DOCTRINES & PRINCIPLES TAUGHT	MY THOUGHTS AND INSIGHTS	ONE PHRASE/PICTURE
24:1-2			
24:3-4			
24:5-7			
24:8-9			
24:10			
24:11-12			
24:13-15			
24:16-18			
25:1-2			
25:3-4			
25:5-6			

3 NEPHI 26 _____
Title for this chapter

In the spaces below, doodle or write about what you learn about each group of verses. At the bottom of each box, come up with a single phrase that encompasses what you learned about that topic.

JESUS EXPOUNDS

V. 1-5

PHRASE:

WHAT THE RECORDS CONTAIN

V. 6-8

PHRASE:

HOW TO RECEIVE GREATER THINGS

V. 9-12

PHRASE:

CHILDREN TEACH

V. 13-14

PHRASE:

WHAT CHRIST DID AS HE MINISTERED

V. 15-16

PHRASE:

ALL THINGS COMMON

V. 17-21

PHRASE:

3 NEPHI 27 _____

Study the following groups of verses; and after you study the verses, pick ONE PHRASE or TEACHING that stands out to you about each topic. Doodle each phrase, and write about what it teaches you in each box below.

CHRIST APPEARS TO THE DISCIPLES **VERSES 1-2**	THE NAME OF CHRIST'S CHURCH **VERSES 3-8**	KEY TO BEING CHRIST'S CHURCH **VERSES 9-10**
BUILT UPON GOSPEL VS. BUILT UPON WORKS OF MEN **VERSES 11-12**	THIS IS THE GOSPEL: **VERSES 13-22**	WRITE THIS... **VERSES 23-26**
BE AS CHRIST **VERSE 27**	FUTURE GENERATIONS **VERSES 28-32**	STRAIT & NARROW **VERSE 33**

3 NEPHI 28 _____

Title for this chapter

As you study this chapter, follow the template below and record what you find in each group of verses: In the first column, doodle or record what is happening and the doctrines and principles being taught. In the second column, record your own thoughts and insights. In the last column, come up with ONE PHRASE or DRAW A PICTURE that portrays an important teaching in those verses.

VERSES	WHAT IS HAPPENING, DOCTRINES & PRINCIPLES TAUGHT	MY THOUGHTS AND INSIGHTS	ONE PHRASE/PICTURE
V. 1-3			
V. 4-6			
V. 7-9			
V. 10-11			
V. 12			
V. 13-15			
V. 16-18			
V. 19-24			
V. 25-28			
V. 29-32			
V. 33-35			
V. 36-38			
V. 39-40			

THREE NEPHITES

THREE NEPHITES

THREE NEPHITES

3 NEPHI 29-30 _____

As you study these chapters, follow the template below and record what you find in each group of verses: In the first column, doodle or record what is happening and the doctrines and principles being taught. In the second column, record your own thoughts and insights. In the last column, come up with ONE PHRASE or DRAW A PICTURE that portrays an important teaching in those verses.

VERSES	WHAT IS HAPPENING, DOCTRINES & PRINCIPLES TAUGHT	MY THOUGHTS AND INSIGHTS	ONE PHRASE / PICTURE
29:1			
29:2-3			
29:4			
29:5			
29:6			
29:7			
29:8			
29:9			
30:1			
30:2			

4 NEPHI 1

ZION ACHIEVED

In 4 Nephi 1, as the people apply the teachings they just received from Christ, they were able to establish Zion. In each box, doodle a picture; or record what is happening, doctrines and principles being taught, something you learn about Zion, or a lesson that stands out to you.

V. 1	V. 2	V. 3
V. 4	V. 5	V. 6
V. 7	V. 8	V. 9
V. 10	V. 11	V. 12
V. 13	V. 14	V. 15
V. 16	V. 17	V. 18

ZION

LOST

In each box, doodle a picture or record what is happening, doctrines and principles being taught, or a lesson that stands out to you. Pay special attention to the things that caused the people to lose Zion.

V. 19–20	V. 21–22	V. 23–24
V. 25–26	V. 27–28	V. 29
V. 30	V. 31	V. 32
V. 33	V. 34	V. 35–36
V. 37–38	V. 39	V. 40–42
V. 43–44	V. 45–47	V. 48–49

MORMON 1 _____

Study each set of verses, and then in each box, record what was happening, write about a doctrine or principle, or record a phrase or a lesson that stands out to you. At the bottom of each box, come up with a phrase that explains the set of verses or a life lesson you learned in those verses.

VERSES 1-2	VERSE 3-4

PHRASE: PHRASE:

VERSES 5-7	VERSE 8-10

PHRASE: PHRASE:

VERSES 11-12	VERSE 13

PHRASE: PHRASE:

VERSES 14	VERSES 15-16

PHRASE: PHRASE:

VERSES 17	VERSES 18-19

PHRASE: PHRASE:

MORMON 2

Title for this chapter

In each box, doodle or record what is happening, doctrines and principles, or a lesson that stands out to you.

MORMON

MORMON HEAD OF AN ARMY	MORMON'S ARMY FRIGHTENED	LAMANITES DRIVE MORMON'S ARMY
V. 1-2	V. 3	V. 4-5

MARCH TOWARDS LAND OF JOSHUA	COMPLETE REVOLUTION	44,000 VS. 42,000	PEOPLE BEGIN TO REPENT
V. 6-7	V. 8	V. 9	V. 10-11

SORROWING NOT UNTO REPENTANCE	REBELLION AGAINST GOD	NEPHITES FLEE AGAIN	MORMON MAKES FULL ACCOUNT ON PLATES
V. 12-13	V. 14-15	V. 16	V. 17-19

CITY OF SHEM	MORMON SPEAKS TO HIS PEOPLE	30,000 VS. 50,000	LAND TREATY
V. 20-22	V. 23-24	V. 25-26	V. 27-29

WHAT ARE SOME LIFE LESSONS YOU CAN LEARN IN THIS CHAPTER?

MORMON 3

Study each set of verses, and then in each box, doodle what was happening, a doctrine or principle, a phrase, an insight, or a lesson that stood out to you.

VERSES 1-3	VERSES 4-8

VERSES 9-13	VERSES 14-16

VERSES 17-19	VERSES 20-22

MORMON 4 _____

Study Mormon 4, and record what happened in the years listed below. Draw pictures, make a list, and record principles you find and lessons learned.

A.D. 363
V. 1-6

A.D. 364-366
V. 7-9

A.D. 367
V. 10-15

A.D. 375
V. 16-23

MORMON 5 _____

Study Mormon 5, and record what happened in the years listed below. Draw pictures, make a list, and record principles you find and lessons learned.

A.D. 375-379
V. 1-5

A.D. 380
V. 6-7

In verses 8-24, Mormon pauses giving a history of the Nephites and offers powerful words meant to be read by us (those who will get this record).   Study those verses and mark important teachings in your scriptures. Once you have finished the chapter, pick two of the teachings you marked and write about them in the space below. Include your own personal thoughts and testimony about each teaching.

ONE

TWO

MORMON 6-7 _____

Title for these chapters

Study Mormon 6, and record what happened in the years listed below. Draw pictures, make a list, record principles you find and lessons learned.

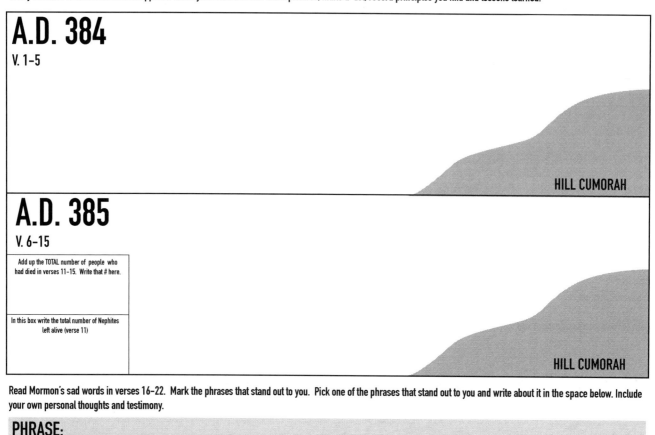

A.D. 384
V. 1-5

HILL CUMORAH

A.D. 385
V. 6-15

Add up the TOTAL number of people who had died in verses 11-15. Write that # here.

In this box write the total number of Nephites left alive (verse 11)

HILL CUMORAH

Read Mormon's sad words in verses 16-22. Mark the phrases that stand out to you. Pick one of the phrases that stand out to you and write about it in the space below. Include your own personal thoughts and testimony.

PHRASE: _____
YOUR PERSONAL THOUGHTS & TESTIMONY:

In chapter 7 Mormon speaks to the Lamanites who will receive the Book of Mormon in the latter days. Read the chapter and mark the important things he says to them. Make a list of 5 important things he said.

1-

2-

3-

4-

5-

MORMON 8 _____
Title for this chapter

As you study this chapter, follow the template below and record what you find in each group of verses: In the first column, doodle or record what is happening and the doctrines and principles being taught. In the second column, record your own thoughts and insights. In the last column, come up with ONE PHRASE, or DRAW A PICTURE that portrays an important teaching in those verses.

VERSES	WHAT IS HAPPENING, DOCTRINES & PRINCIPLES TAUGHT	MY THOUGHTS AND INSIGHTS	ONE PHRASE/PICTURE
V. 1-3	TIP: Moroni takes over the records from Mormon		
V. 4-5			
V. 6-8			
V. 9-11			
V. 12-14			
V. 15-17			
V. 18-21			
V. 22-24			
V. 25-28			
V. 29-32			
V. 33-35			
V. 36-38			
V. 39-41			

MORMON 9 _____

Title for this chapter

As you study this chapter, follow the template below and record what you find in each group of verses: In the first column, doodle or record what is happening and the doctrines and principles being taught. In the second column, record your own thoughts and insights. In the last column, come up with ONE PHRASE, or DRAW A PICTURE that portrays an important teaching in those verses.

VERSES	WHAT IS HAPPENING, DOCTRINES & PRINCIPLES TAUGHT	MY THOUGHTS AND INSIGHTS	ONE PHRASE/PICTURE
V. 1-2			
V. 3-6			
V. 7-8			
V. 9-10			
V. 11-12			
V. 13-14			
V. 15-17			
V. 18-20			
V. 21-25			
V. 26-27			
V. 28-30			
V. 31-34			
V. 35-37			

127

ETHER 1 _____

As you study this chapter, follow the template below and record what you find in each group of verses: In the first column, doodle or record what is happening and the doctrines and principles being taught. In the second column, record your own thoughts and insights. In the last column, come up with ONE PHRASE, or DRAW A PICTURE that portrays an important teaching in those verses.

VERSES	WHAT IS HAPPENING, DOCTRINES & PRINCIPLES TAUGHT	MY THOUGHTS AND INSIGHTS	ONE PHRASE/PICTURE
V. 1-2	TIP: REFER TO YOUR NOTES FOR MOSIAH 8:7-11 TO REFRESH YOUR MEMORY OF THE 24 PLATES. MORONI WOULD HAVE HAD THESE PLATES PASSED DOWN TO HIM.		
V. 3-5			
V. 6-32			
V. 33-34			
V. 35			
V. 36			
V. 37			
V. 38			
V. 39-40			
V. 41			
V. 42			
V. 43			

ETHER 2

Study each set of verses, and then in each box, record or draw what was happening. You can also write about a doctrine or principle or record a phrase or a lesson that stands out to you. At the bottom of each box, come up with a life lesson you can learn from those verses.

VERSES 1–3	VERSES 4–7

LIFE LESSON: | LIFE LESSON:

VERSES 8–12	VERSE 13

LIFE LESSON: | LIFE LESSON:

VERSES 14–15	VERSES 16–17

LIFE LESSON: | LIFE LESSON:

VERSES 18–21	VERSES 22–25

LIFE LESSON: | LIFE LESSON:

129

ETHER 3

In each box, doodle or record what is happening, doctrines and principles, or a lesson that stands out to you.

SIXTEEN SMALL STONES	BROTHER OF JARED'S PRAYER	BROTHER OF JARED'S PRAYER	THE LORD'S HAND
V. 1	V. 2-3	V. 4-5	V. 6

THE BROTHER OF JARED IS AFRAID	BECAUSE OF THY FAITH	JARED'S REQUEST	THE LORD'S QUESTION
V. 7-8	V. 9	V. 10	V. 11-12

THE LORD SHOWS HIMSELF	"I AM HE"	TIP: This quote may help you understand verse 15.	"NEVER HAVE I SHOWED MYSELF..."
V. 13	V. 14	"[When Christ said], 'Never have I showed myself unto man whom I have created,' He was saying to the brother of Jared, 'Never have I showed myself unto man in this manner, without my volition, driven solely by the faith of the beholder.' As a rule, prophets are invited into the presence of the Lord.... Obviously the Lord Himself was linking unprecedented faith with this unprecedented vision." ELDER JEFFREY R. HOLLAND Christ and the New Covenant, 23	V. 15

BODY OF SPIRIT	THE LORD MINISTERED UNTO HIM	HE KNEW, NOTHING DOUBTING	SHOW TO NO MAN
V. 16	V. 17-18	V. 19-20	V. 21

SEAL THEM UP	TWO STONES	A VISION	WRITE AND SEAL
V. 22	V. 23-24	V. 25-26	V. 27-28

ETHER 4 _____

Title for this chapter

Study each set of verses, and then in each box, record or draw what was happening. You can also write about a doctrine or principle or record a phrase or a lesson that stands out to you. At the bottom of each box, come up with a life lesson you can learn from those verses.

MORONI TO SEAL UP THE BROTHER OF JARED'S WRITINGS	WRITINGS SHALL NOT GO FORTH UNTIL MEN HAVE SUFFICIENT FAITH
VERSES 1-5	VERSES 6-7
LIFE LESSON:	LIFE LESSON:
WARNING FOR THOSE WHO DO NOT BELIEVE THE WORD OF THE LORD	PROMISE TO THOSE WHO BELIEVE THE WORD OF THE LORD
VERSES 8-10	VERSE 11-12
LIFE LESSON:	LIFE LESSON:
COME UNTO CHRIST	SIGNS
VERSES 13-15	VERSES 16-17
LIFE LESSON:	LIFE LESSON:
SIGNS FOLLOW BELIEVERS	BLESSED IS HE
VERSE 18	VERSES 19
LIFE LESSON:	LIFE LESSON:

ETHER 5 _____

PROPHECY OF THE THREE WITNESSES
Write or draw at least one doctrine or principle taught in each verse below.

V. 1	V. 2	V. 3
V. 4	V. 5	V. 6

1. What was Joseph Smith able to do according to verses 2 and 3?

2. Who were the three witnesses to the Book of Mormon? (For help, refer to "The Testimony of the Three Witnesses" at the front of the Book of Mormon.)

   ❶

   ❷

   ❸

3. What are some specific prophecies given about the testiomny of the three witnesses? (Verses 3–4)

ETHER 6

_____

Title for this chapter

VERSES 1-3	VERSE 4
Read verses 1-3. Explain this picture.	Read verse 4. Consider specific things the Jaredites would have packed. Make a packing list on this scroll.

VERSES 5-8	VERSES 9-11
Explain this picture after you study verses 5-8. At the bottom of this box, write about a life lesson we can learn from these verses.	Ponder verses 9-11. Think of a principle in those scriptures that can help us in our lives today. Write about it in this box.

LIFE LESSON:

VERSE 12	VERSES 13-20
Study verse 12. Consider the "tender mercies" they would have received. Write about them in this box.	Study verses 13-18. Write about, or draw, what you learn in those verses.

Tender Mercies

JARED

BROTHER OF JARED

VERSES 21-26	VERSES 27-28
Make a list of the key events that occurred in verses 21-26.	Write what you learn about Orihah and what happened while he was king.

ORIHAH

IF YOU WERE ASKED TO GIVE A TALK AT CHURCH ABOUT ETHER 6, WHAT WOULD YOU CALL YOUR TALK, AND WHAT WOULD YOU TALK ABOUT?

ETHER 7

_____
Title for this chapter

Doodle on this illustration what is happening in the verses given in the black boxes. Include additional pictures, your insights, and personal commentary.

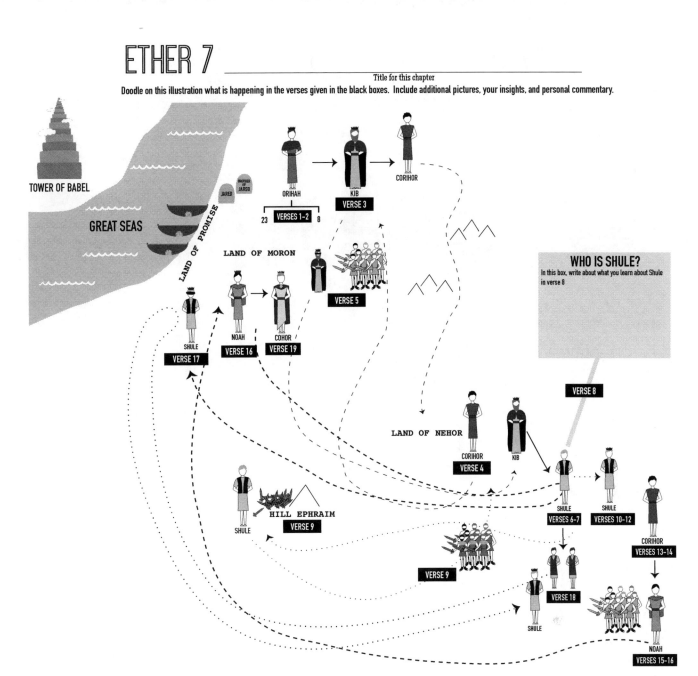

TOWER OF BABEL

GREAT SEAS

LAND OF PROMISE

JARED BROTHER OF JARED

ORIHAH
23 | VERSES 1-2 | 8

KIB
VERSE 3

CORIHOR

LAND OF MORON

NOAH
VERSE 16

COHOR
VERSE 19

SHULE
VERSE 17

VERSE 5

WHO IS SHULE?
In this box, write about what you learn about Shule in verse 8

VERSE 8

LAND OF NEHOR

CORIHOR
VERSE 4

KIB

SHULE
VERSES 6-7

SHULE
VERSES 10-12

CORIHOR
VERSES 13-14

HILL EPHRAIM
VERSE 9

SHULE

VERSE 9

VERSE 18

SHULE

NOAH
VERSES 15-16

V. 20 What happened to the Jaredites when Shule and Cohor were kings?	**V. 21** What did Cohor attempt to do? What ended up happening instead?
V. 22 Who was Nimrod and what did he do? NIMROD	**V. 23** What important things do you learn in this verse?
V. 24 How did the Jaredites treat the prophets?	**V. 25** What law did the king execute and what did it cause to happen?
V. 26 What important things do you learn in this verse?	**V. 27** What is the state of the Jaredites at the end of this chapter?

This chapter covers seven generations and crucial events that happened during those generations. How would you explain the seven generations in a few sentences?

ETHER 8 _____

Doodle on this illustration what is happening in the verses given in the black boxes. Include additional pictures, your insights, and personal commentary.

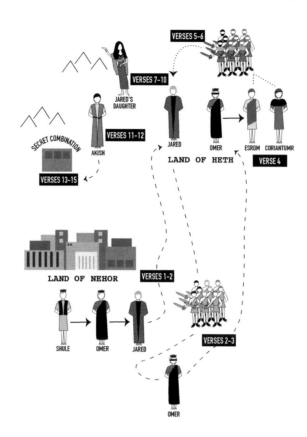

SECRET COMBINATIONS:
Study verses 15-26 in your scriptures. Mark everything you learn about secret combinations. In the space below write about 5 of the things you learned in those scriptures.

ONE:

TWO:

THREE:

FOUR:

FIVE:

ETHER 9 _____

Title for this chapter

Doodle on this illustration what is happening in the verses given in the black boxes. Include additional pictures, your insights, and personal commentary.

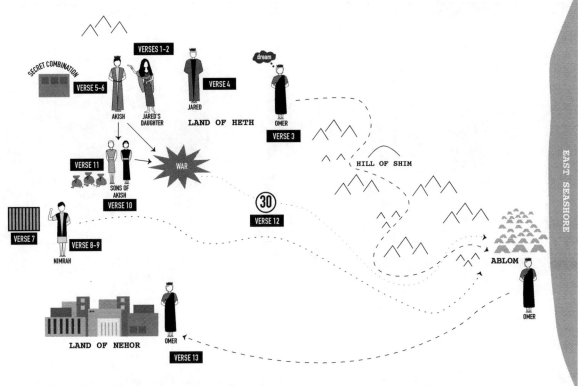

Study each set of verses. In each box, record what is happening and insights and principles you find.

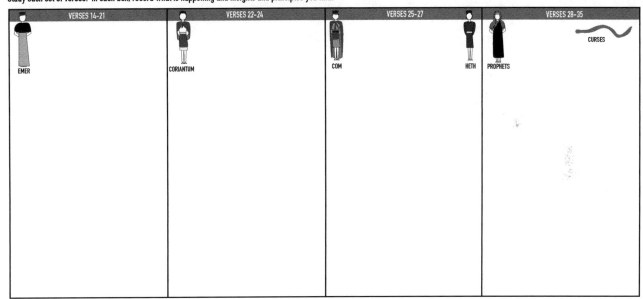

VERSES 14-21	VERSES 22-24	VERSES 25-27	VERSES 28-35
EMER	CORIANTUM	COM	HETH / PROPHETS / CURSES

LESSONS LEARNED Write about some important life lessons you found in this chapter.

ETHER 10 _____

Title for this chapter

Each of the boxes below covers a reign of a Jaredite king. Study each set of verses. In each box, record what is happening and insights and principles you find. If the king was a righteous king, check the box next to "righteous". If he was wicked, check the box next to "wicked".

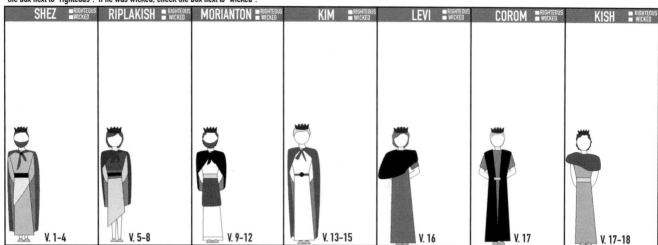

SHEZ ▪RIGHTEOUS ▪WICKED	RIPLAKISH ▪RIGHTEOUS ▪WICKED	MORIANTON ▪RIGHTEOUS ▪WICKED	KIM ▪RIGHTEOUS ▪WICKED	LEVI ▪RIGHTEOUS ▪WICKED	COROM ▪RIGHTEOUS ▪WICKED	KISH ▪RIGHTEOUS ▪WICKED
V. 1-4	V. 5-8	V. 9-12	V. 13-15	V. 16	V. 17	V. 17-18

This box is about the reign of King Lib. Use the story map to illustrate or write about what happened while he was king.

WEST SEASHORE

LAND OF MORON

LAND OF HETH

HILL OF SHIM

LAND OF NEHOR

HILL EPHRAIM

ABLOM

EAST SEASHORE

KING LIB V. 19-29

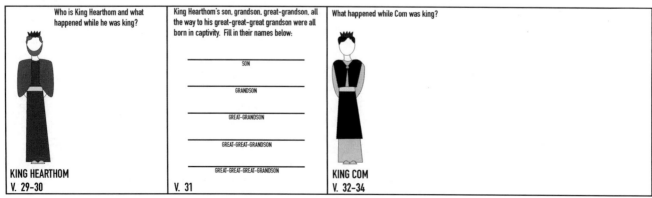

Who is King Hearthom and what happened while he was king?

KING HEARTHOM
V. 29-30

King Hearthom's son, grandson, great-grandson, all the way to his great-great-great grandson were all born in captivity. Fill in their names below:

_____
SON

_____
GRANDSON

_____
GREAT-GRANDSON

_____
GREAT-GREAT-GRANDSON

_____
GREAT-GREAT-GREAT-GRANDSON

V. 31

What happened while Com was king?

KING COM
V. 32-34

ETHER 11 _____

(Title for this chapter)

Each of the boxes below covers the descendants in the royal line. Study each set of verses. In each box, record what happened while each man lived. In the box at the end, record a life lesson or important principle you found in those verses. Some of the men below are unfinished; have some fun finishing the pictures. If he was a righteous man, check the box next to "righteous". If he was wicked, check the box next to "wicked".

COM
V. 1-3

☐ RIGHTEOUS
☐ WICKED
☐ UNKNOWN

SHIBLOM
V. 4-9

☐ RIGHTEOUS
☐ WICKED
☐ UNKNOWN

SETH
V. 9

☐ RIGHTEOUS
☐ WICKED
☐ UNKNOWN

AHAH
V. 10

☐ RIGHTEOUS
☐ WICKED
☐ UNKNOWN

ETHEM
V. 11-14

☐ RIGHTEOUS
☐ WICKED
☐ UNKNOWN

MORON
V. 14-18

☐ RIGHTEOUS
☐ WICKED
☐ UNKNOWN

CORIANTOR
V. 19-22

ETHER
V. 11:23, 12:1-5

TIP: Ether would have been a king if the crown had not been lost in his family line. This Ether is the prophet whom the Book of Ether is named after.

138

ETHER 12:1-22 _____

In this chapter, the prophet Ether teaches the people; and Moroni takes the opportunity to teach us about "faith".

1. Look over verses 6–22, and circle every time you find the word "faith". Count them and write that number here: _____.
2. Study these verses, and mark the phrases and teachings that stand out to you.
3. Choose five of the teachings or phrases you marked, and write about each of them in the spaces below.

TEACHING / PHRASE	VERSE	THOUGHTS / INSIGHTS
ONE		
TWO		
THREE		
FOUR		
FIVE		

ETHER 12:23-41 _____

Title for these verses

Study each set of verses, and then in each box, record, doodle, or diagram what Moroni is teaching. At the bottom of each box, come up with a life lesson you can learn from those verses.

VERSES 23-25	VERSES 26-27

LIFE LESSON: | LIFE LESSON:

VERSES 28-29	VERSES 30-31

LIFE LESSON: | LIFE LESSON:

VERSES 32-33	VERSES 34-35

LIFE LESSON: | LIFE LESSON:

VERSES 36-37	VERSES 38-41

LIFE LESSON: | LIFE LESSON:

ETHER 13

Title for this chapter

ETHER

Ether taught the people some very important teachings. In the spaces below, doodle, diagram, or record what you learn from Ether about the topics in each box.

NEW JERUSALEM
V. 1–10

OLD JERUSALEM
V. 11–12

As you study the rest of chapter 13, doodle what you learn in the boxes below. Include what is happening, doctrines and principles you find, and your own personal thoughts and insights.

V. 13–14	
V. 15	
V. 16–17	
V. 18–19	
V. 20–21	
V. 22	
V. 23–24	
V. 25–26	
V. 27–29	
V. 30–31	

CORIANTUMR

ETHER 14

Title for this chapter

TIP: The Jaredite civilization existed for over 2,000 years. The Nephite civilization lasted under 1,000 years. Although Ether is a small book, it is a record of an enormous civilization. Mormon reduced their history into a mere 15 chapters and focused mainly on important events that occurred during the kings' reigns, along with some of the warnings from the many prophets. We know that they were a civilized and industrious people (see Ether 10:22-28). Instead of finding out about specific cities, we are told, "they began to spread upon the face of the land" (Ether 6:18).

The story map below is just to give you an idea of the events as the Jaredite civilization came to an end. However, that map is likely just a portion of the actual size of the Jaredite civilization.

Use the boxes below to record what is happening, and what you learn from each verse in this chapter. Use the story map below to doodle events on to help you imagine what the Jaredites experienced.

V. 1-2	V. 3-4	V. 5-6
V. 7-8	V. 9-10	V. 11-12
V. 13-15	V. 16-17	V. 18-20
V. 21-23	V. 24	V. 25
V. 26-27	V. 28-29	V. 30-31

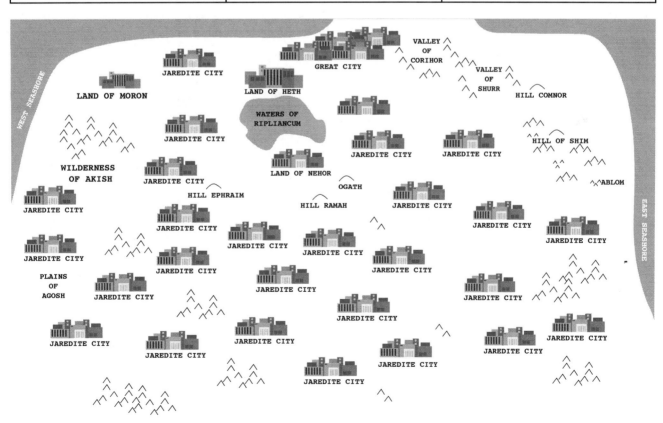

142

ETHER 15

Title for this chapter

Study each set of verses, and then in each box, record what is happening, a phrase, insights, or a lesson that stood out to you.

CORIANTUMR BEGINS TO REMEMBER	CORIANTUMR TRIES TO NEGOTIATE WITH SHIZ	BATTLE	CORIANTUMR'S ARMY FLEES
V. 1–3	V. 4–5	V. 6	V. 7–8

EXCEEDINGLY SORE BATTLE	ALL PEOPLE GATHER	ALL PEOPLE FIGHT	GREAT LOSS
V. 9–11	V. 12–14	V. 15	V. 16–17

SATAN HAD FULL POWER OVER HEARTS	FEW NUMBERS LEFT	EVEN FEWER NUMBERS LEFT	FINAL BATTLE
V. 18–19	V. 20–23	V. 24–25	V. 26–27

ALL FALLEN	CORIANTUMR IS ONLY SURVIVOR	ETHER FINISHES RECORD	ETHER'S LAST WORDS
V. 28–29	V. 30–32	V. 33	V. 34

LESSONS
FROM THE
BOOK OF ETHER
Write about some of the lessons, thoughts, and insights you have gained from the Book of Ether and the story of the Jaredites.

MORONI 1 _____
Title for this chapter

1. What do you think Moroni's experience might have been like as he abridged the Jaredite records?

2. What messages do you think Moroni would want us to learn from the records of the Jaredite civilization and the Nephite civilization?

Study verses 1–4 in Moroni 1. In the boxes below, record what you learn about Moroni or his civilization. Include some of your thoughts about what Moroni might have been experiencing on a personal level.

VERSE 1	VERSE 2
VERSE 3	**VERSE 4**

MORONI 2-3 _____

With time still left on earth, Moroni adds to the plates; and in chapters 2–6, he teaches about essential ordinances. In the boxes below, record everything you learn from Moroni about the following ordinances. Add your thoughts about why you think Moroni thought it was important for us to know these details.

ORDINANCE OF CONFIRMATION
MORONI 2:1–3

PRIESTHOOD ORDINATION
MORONI 3:1–4

MORONI 4-6 _____

Title for these chapters

With time still left on earth, Moroni adds to the plates; and in chapters 2-6, he teaches about essential ordinances. In the boxes below, record everything you learn from Moroni about the following ordinances. Add your thoughts about why you think Moroni thought it was important for us to know these details.

THE SACRAMENTAL BREAD
MORONI 4:1-3

THE SACRAMENTAL WINES
MORONI 5:1-2

BAPTISM
MORONI 6:1-4

CHURCH MEETINGS
MORONI 6:5-9

147

MORONI 7 _____

VERSES 1-5	VERSES 6-7

LIFE LESSON: | LIFE LESSON:

VERSES 8-11	VERSES 12-15

LIFE LESSON: | LIFE LESSON:

VERSES 16-17	VERSES 18-22

LIFE LESSON: | LIFE LESSON:

VERSES 23-25	VERSES 26-28

LIFE LESSON: | LIFE LESSON:

VERSES 29–31	VERSES 32–35
LIFE LESSON:	LIFE LESSON:

VERSES 36–39	VERSES 40–42
LIFE LESSON:	LIFE LESSON:

VERSES 43–44	VERSE 45
LIFE LESSON:	LIFE LESSON:

VERSES 46–47	VERSE 48
LIFE LESSON:	LIFE LESSON:

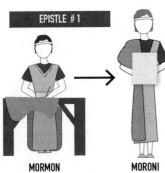

MORMON   MORONI

MORONI 8

_____
Title for this chapter

1. What do you learn about this chapter in verse 1?

2. What is special about Mormon's opening statements in his letter to his son? (See verses 2 and 3)

3. Mormon has learned that there have been doctrinal disagreements. What doctrine had Moroni and others disagreed about? (See verses 4-6)

4. What did Mormon do in order to correct this issue? (See verse 7)

5. Mormon fills his letter with correct doctrine about baptism and the need for little children to be baptized. In each box below, record at least one doctrine or principle you learn from each verse.

V. 8	
V. 9	
V. 10	
V. 11	
V. 12	
V. 13	
V. 14-15	
V. 16	
V. 17-18	
V. 19-20	
V. 21	
V. 22-23	
V. 24	
V. 25-26	
V. 27-28	
V. 29-30	

MORONI 9

Title for this chapter

MORMON → MORONI

VERSES 1-3

Doodle or write about the state of the Nephites in these verses.

VERSES 4-6

Doodle or write about what Mormon teaches in these verses.

VERSES 7-10

Study these verses, and then come up with 5 words that describe the suffering of the people. Doodle them below.

ONE	TWO	THREE	FOUR	FIVE

VERSES 11-24

Study these verses, and doodle or write about the concerns, warnings, and teachings Mormon shared with Moroni.

VERSES 25-26

Pick a phrase from Moroni's farewell words to his son. Doodle that phrase and write about them below.

MORONI 10

As you study this chapter, doodle or write answers to the following questions.

HOW CAN I KNOW WHAT IS GOOD AND TRUE?	WHAT ARE THE GIFTS OF THE SPIRIT?

WHY IS FAITH, HOPE, & CHARITY IMPORTANT?	WHY IS IT IMPORTANT FOR ME TO STUDY THE WORDS OF PROPHETS WHO LIVED SO LONG AGO?

WHAT CAN I DO TO COME UNTO CHRIST?	FAVORITE PHRASE
	Pick your favorite phrase from this chapter and doodle and write about it in this box.

MY TESTIMONY OF THE BOOK OF MORMON

NOW THAT YOU HAVE COMPLETED A CAREFUL AND MEANINGFUL STUDY OF THE BOOK OF MORMON, WRITE ABOUT YOUR OWN TESTIMONY ABOUT THE POWER OF THIS BOOK AND SOME SPECIFIC LESSONS THAT HAVE STOOD OUT TO YOU.

MY COMMENTARY

As you are studying the Book of Mormon and have thoughts you would like to record, use these pages to record your valuable insights. Use the left column to record the page and scripture you were studying and are now writing about. You may only write a few sentences or you may write several pages of your own commentary. After you have finished writing, go back to the pages you were originally studying and make a note on the bottom of the page that you have written commentary in the back of this book. For example you may write: "My commentary on page 118".

SCRIPTURE/
PAGE

MY COMMENTARY

MY COMMENTARY

SCRIPTURE/
PAGE

MY COMMENTARY

SCRIPTURE/
PAGE

MY COMMENTARY

MY COMMENTARY

MY COMMENTARY

MY COMMENTARY

MY COMMENTARY

SCRIPTURE/
PAGE

MY COMMENTARY

MY COMMENTARY

SCRIPTURE/
PAGE

MY COMMENTARY

SCRIPTURE/
PAGE

MY COMMENTARY

SCRIPTURE/
PAGE

MY COMMENTARY

MY COMMENTARY

MY COMMENTARY

SCRIPTURE/
PAGE

MY COMMENTARY

SCRIPTURE/
PAGE

MY COMMENTARY

SCRIPTURE/
PAGE

MY COMMENTARY

SCRIPTURE/
PAGE

MY COMMENTARY

SCRIPTURE/
PAGE

MY COMMENTARY

MY COMMENTARY

SCRIPTURE/
PAGE

Made in the USA
San Bernardino, CA
05 October 2015